INDIVIDUALISED MATHEMATICS

Developed by the School Mathematics Project in association with the National Extension College

**ALGEBRA 1
LANGUAGE AND STRUCTURE**

CAMBRIDGE UNIVERSITY PRESS

Cambridge
London   New York   New Rochelle
Melbourne   Sydney

The School Mathematics Project

When the SMP was founded in 1961, its main objective was to devise radically new secondary school mathematics courses to reflect, more adequately than did the traditional syllabuses, the up-to-date nature and usages of mathematics.

SMP Books 1–5 form a five-year course leading to the O-level examination in SMP Mathematics. *Revised Advanced Mathematics Books 1, 2 and 3* cover the syllabus for the A-level examination in SMP Mathematics. Five shorter texts cover the material of the various sections of the A-level examination SMP Further Mathematics. There are two books for SMP Additional Mathematics at O-level. All the SMP GCE examinations are available to schools through any of the GCE examining boards.

Books A–H cover broadly the same development of mathematics as the first few books of the O-level series. Most CSE boards offer appropriate examinations. In practice, this series is being used very widely across all streams of comprehensive schools and its first seven books, together with *Books X, Y and Z*, provide a course leading to the SMP O-level examination. *SMP Cards I and II* provide an alternative treatment in card form of the mathematics in *Books A–D*. The six units of *SMP 7–13*, designed for children in that age-range, provide a course for middle schools which is also widely used in primary schools and the first two years of secondary schools. Teacher's guides accompany all these series.

The SMP has produced many other texts, and teachers are encouraged to obtain each year from the Cambridge University Press, P.O. Box 110, Cambridge CB2 3RL, the full list of SMP publications currently available. In the same way, help and advice may always be sought by teachers from the Executive Director at the SMP Office, Westfield College, Kidderpore Avenue, London NW3 7ST. The annual Reports, details of forthcoming in-service training courses and other information may be obtained from the SMP Office.

The SMP is continually evaluating old work and preparing for new. The effectiveness of the SMP's work depends, as it has always done, on the comments and reactions received from teachers and pupils in a wide variety of schools using SMP materials. Readers of the texts can, therefore, send their comments to the SMP in the knowledge that they will be taken into consideration.

The authors of the original books on whose work this series is based are named in *The School Mathematics Project: The First Ten Years*, published by the Cambridge University Press.

SMP Individualised Mathematics has been produced by a team consisting of

>   Judy Bonsall   G. Merlane
>   G. S. Howlett   L. Savins
>   M. K. Leach   D. R. Skinner
>   J. L. Lloyd   J. V. Tyson

John Lloyd led the work on the series until his death in 1977, and the final editing has been carried out by Derek Skinner. Many others have helped with advice and criticism, particularly those students who worked through the material in draft form.

Contents

Preface	*page*	v
How to use this book		vi

1 Set language   1
    Objectives   1
    Pre-test   1
  1.1 Set notation   1
  1.2 Subsets   4
  1.3 The universal set   6
  1.4 Venn diagrams   6
    Summary   8
    Post-test   9
    Assignment   10
    Answers   11

2 Relations   16
    Objectives   16
    Pre-test   16
  2.1 Mapping machines   17
  2.2 Relations   18
  2.3 Mappings   20
  2.4 Different types of relations   21
  2.5 Inverse relations   23
    Summary   25
    Post-test   26
    Assignment   27
    Answers   27

3 Functions   35
    Objectives   35
    Pre-test   35
  3.1 Functions   36
  3.2 Function notation   38

	3.3	Flow diagrams for composite functions	39
	3.4	Inverse functions	40
	3.5	Self-inverse functions	41
		Summary	43
		Post-test	43
		Assignment	44
		Answers	44
4	**Combining sets and combining functions**		49
		Objectives	49
		Pre-test	49
	4.1	Intersection of sets	50
	4.2	Union of sets	51
	4.3	The number of elements in sets and subsets	52
	4.4	Composite functions	55
	4.5	Inverses of composite functions	57
		Summary	60
		Post-test	61
		Assignment	62
		Answers	62
5	**Mathematical structure**		74
		Objectives	74
		Pre-test	74
	5.1	Elements, operations and relations	75
	5.2	Commutativity, associativity and closure	78
	5.3	Identity and inverse elements	80
	5.4	The distributive law, and further developments	85
		Summary	87
		Post-test	88
		Assignment	89
		Answers	90

Preface

SMP Individualised Mathematics is based upon the content of *SMP Books 1–5* and *Books A–G, X, Y, Z*, covering the syllabus for the O-level SMP Mathematics.

There are two main distinguishing features of the series. First, the material is presented in a programmed form and the books are thus suitable for use in individualised learning, where self-assessment and clear explanation play a major role. The carefully structured development of each topic makes the books suitable for use by students working alone with minimum tuition, in schools, technical colleges, colleges of further education and on courses organised by the National Extension College.

Secondly, instead of the spiral development of the SMP texts, *SMP Individualised Mathematics* presents the mathematics by topics. Each book, apart from the two devoted to revision, presents the work on a particular theme. Hence the books will prove useful to pupils who have missed work through absence from class, to students coming from abroad, and to pupils transferring to a different school. The style and arrangement of these books should make them very suitable for use by pupils in the sixth form who are working to improve their earlier performance at CSE or O-level. The books will also be useful for revision and consolidation.

Although written with the SMP O-level course in mind, *SMP Individualised Mathematics*, like other SMP texts, can be used to prepare for other O-level examinations based on similar syllabuses.

The titles in this series are as follows:
- Computation and Graphs
- Probability and Statistics
- *Algebra 1: Language and Structure*
- *Algebra 2: Equations, Formulas and Graphs*
- *Further Algebra and Computation*
- *Matrix Algebra and Isometric Transformations*
- *Further Matrices and Transformations*
- Geometry 1: Symmetry and Trigonometry
- Geometry 2: Shapes and Similarity
- Geometry 3: Three Dimensions
- Revision 1
- Revision 2

How to use this book

Each chapter begins with a list of what you should be able to do after studying the chapter. This is followed by a pre-test, which gives you some idea of what you should know before you start that particular chapter. If you have difficulty with the pre-test, you should revise the work required for it – from either the appropriate chapter of this or a companion book, or an elementary text-book – before continuing with the chapter.

The teaching part of the chapter is divided into several numbered sections, and includes a number of exercises. Other questions are asked in the text, and *you should write down the answers to all these questions and exercises in a notebook* as you go along. The start of each set of questions is marked by a white triangle on the left-hand side of the page. When you come to a triangle with a number in it (on the *right-hand* side of the page) you should check your work to that point by turning to the answers at the end of the chapter and finding the triangle with the same number (now on the *left-hand* side of the page).

The teaching part of the chapter is followed by a summary of the important results of the chapter (you may well find it helpful to copy these into a separate notebook that is kept especially for revision), and a post-test to test your understanding of the chapter as a whole. The answers to this post-test are also at the end of the chapter.

Finally (apart from the answers) there is an 'assignment'. This is another exercise covering the whole chapter, but this time there are no answers in this book. If at all possible you should have *this* exercise marked by a teacher or tutor.

1 Set language

Objectives

This is what you should be able to do after studying this chapter.
(1) Define a set and list its elements (or members).
(2) Determine whether or not an element belongs to a particular set.
(3) Recognise subsets, proper subsets and equal sets.
(4) Select an appropriate universal set for a given situation.
(5) Obtain the complement of a given set for a given universal set.
(6) Use Venn diagrams.
(7) Identify, and use correctly, the following symbols.
$\{\}, \subset, \not\subset, \supset, \not\supset, \in, \notin, A', :, \mathscr{E}$

Pre-test

1   (a)   What is a prime number?
       (b)   Write down the list of prime numbers less than 30.

2   Write down six multiples of 3 that are less than 100.

3   (a)   What is a quadrilateral?
       (b)   Write down the names of four special types of quadrilaterals.

4   What does $0 < x \leqslant 8$ mean?

1.1 Set notation

We are all familiar with collective names. Phrases like a *herd* of cattle, a *bunch* of flowers, and a *fleet* of ships are quite common. In mathematics, too, we often need to talk about collections of things. For example, we might need to talk about
(a) the whole numbers between 10 and 20,
(b) the shapes with four straight sides, or
(c) the letters used in spelling the word *mathematical*.

    The mathematical name for a collection of things is a *set*. Each thing belonging to a particular set is a *member* or *element* of that set. For example, 13 is an element of (belongs to) set (a).

▷ 1 Give two elements of each of the sets (*b*) and (*c*).

When we list or count the elements of a set, all the elements must be different. For example, in set (*c*) the letters *a*, *m* and *t* are each counted once only, so set (*c*) contains the eight elements *a*, *c*, *e*, *h*, *i*, *l*, *m* and *t*. When we list the elements of a set, we put curly brackets { } around the list to show that we are thinking of it as a set. So set (*c*) is written as {*a*, *c*, *e*, *h*, *i*, *l*, *m*, *t*}. The order of the elements in the list does not matter, so set (*c*) could just as well be written as {*m*, *a*, *t*, *h*, *e*, *i*, *c*, *l*}.

Two sets containing the same elements are equal. For example, {*a*, *c*, *e*} = {*c*, *e*, *a*}.

2 How many elements are there in set (*a*) and in set (*b*)?

3 Write out set (*a*) using curly brackets.

To avoid writing a full description every time we want to refer to a set, we use capital letters as 'names' for sets. For instance, set (*a*) above might be called *S*, so that
$$S = \{\text{whole numbers between 10 and 20}\}.$$

Note that we do not put curly brackets around *S*, but whenever we describe a set by any other method curly brackets must be used.

When we describe a set we must make it absolutely clear what does and what does not belong to the set. When this is done, the set is said to be *well-defined*.

4 (*a*) Why is 'the set of tall people' not well-defined?
 (*b*) Is set (*b*) well-defined?

A set like *S* can be defined in three different ways, as follows:

In words, as in
$$S = \{\text{whole numbers between 10 and 20}\}.$$

(This is read as 'the set of whole numbers between 10 and 20'.)

By listing the elements, as in
$$S = \{11, 12, 13, 14, 15, 16, 17, 18, 19\}.$$

(This reads 'the set containing the elements 11, 12, ..., 19'.)

By giving a 'formula' from which every element can be listed, as in
$$S = \{x: 10 < x < 20, \text{ where } x \text{ is an integer}\}.$$

(Literally, this reads 'the set of numbers *x* such that *x* lies between 10 and 20, where *x* is an integer'. The curly brackets are read as 'the set of' and the colon 'such that'. In practice, we usually shorten this to 'the set of integers *x* which are greater than 10 but less than 20'.)

▷ 5 List the elements of these sets.
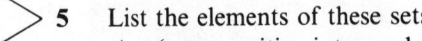
A = {even positive integers less than 12}
B = {colours of the rainbow}

It is convenient to have a symbol to stand for 'is a member of' (or 'belongs to'). The symbol used is ∈. Thus, for the set *S* = {integers between 10 and 20}, $13 \in S$. In a similar way, ∉ means 'is not a member of'. Thus, $13 \notin A$ for the set *A* = {even positive integers less than 12}.

6 Using the sets *A* and *S* as defined above, copy and complete these.
 (*a*) 10 □ *A*   (*b*) 10 □ *S*   (*c*) 15 ∈ □   (*d*) 12 ∉ □

Some sets have too many elements to be listed individually. Consider
$P = \{\text{whole numbers between 0 and 1000}\}$,
$Q = \{\text{counting numbers}\}$.

If we want to list the elements of such sets, we list the first few until it is clear what the pattern is, then put three dots, and finally the last element (if there is one). So, for example,
$P = \{1, 2, 3, \ldots, 999\}$,
$Q = \{0, 1, 2, 3, \ldots\}$.

7 List the members of these sets.
$C = \{\text{even numbers between 0 and 500}\}$
$D = \{\text{multiples of 5 greater than 0}\}$

8 Describe these sets.
$E = \{1, 4, 9, 16, \ldots\}$
$F = \{101, 103, 105, \ldots, 199\}$

9 How would you list the following set Z?
$Z = \{\text{integers}\} = \{\text{whole numbers; positive, zero and negative}\}$

Exercise A

1 List the members of these sets.
 (a) {positive numbers less than 20 that are divisible by 3}
 (b) {the five senses}
 (c) $\{x : x+3 = 5\}$
 (d) {counting numbers greater than 100}
 (e) $\{x : x \leqslant 8, x \text{ is a positive integer}\}$

2 Describe these sets.
 (a) $\{a, e, i, o, u\}$
 (b) $\{1, 3, 5, 7, \ldots\}$
 (c) {hearts, clubs, spades, diamonds}
 (d) $\{2, 3, 5, 7, 11, 13, 17, 19\}$
 (e) $\{\ldots, {}^-4, {}^-2, 0, 2, 4, 6, \ldots\}$

3 List the members of these sets.
$A = \{\text{odd numbers between 0 and 10}\}$
$B = \{\text{square numbers}\}$
$C = \{x : 6 < x \leqslant 16, x \text{ is an integer}\}$
Deduce the value (or values) of x for each of these cases.
 (a) $x \in A$ and $x \in B$
 (b) $x \in B$ and $x \in C$
 (c) $x \in A, x \in B$ and $x \in C$
 (d) $x \in A$ but $x \notin C$
 (e) $x \notin A$ and $x \notin B$ but $x \in C$

4 Write these in set notation.
 (a) 169 is a square number.
 (b) d is not a vowel.
 (c) 6 belongs to the set of even numbers that are greater than 2 but less than 22.

5   Which of the following sets are not well-defined? Explain why.
    (a) {coral reefs off Tobago}
    (b) {sunny days in Huddersfield in March 1980}
    (c) {bank holidays in England}

1.2 Subsets

1   (a) List the members of these sets.
        $A = \{$factors of 16$\}$
        $B = \{$factors of 48$\}$
    (b) Do you notice any connection between the sets A and B?

In cases like this, when every member of a set A is also a member of a set B, we say that A is a *subset* of B. This is written $A \subset B$. We can also write $B \supset A$ (the set B contains all the elements of set A) but it is less common to express the connection this way round.

Note the difference between the symbols $\in$ and $\subset$. The symbol $\in$ shows that an *element* belongs to a set, as in $13 \in \{$primes$\}$. However, $\subset$ shows that a *set* belongs to, or is contained in, another set, as in $\{11, 13, 17\} \subset \{$prime numbers$\}$.

2   Is B a subset of A? Or can you find a member of B that is not a member of A?

We can use $\not\subset$ to stand for 'is not a subset of', and so we can write $B \not\subset A$ (and $A \not\supset B$, 'the set B is not contained in the set A'). In these cases, there is at least one member of B that does not belong to the set A.

We can use this last idea if we want to show that any set (C, say) is not a subset of another set (D, say). All we have to do is find, as a *counter-example*, an element of C which is not an element of D.

3   If P and Q are sets such that $P \subset Q$ and $Q \subset P$, what can you say about them?

4   Are the following true or false? Give a counter-example if they are false.
    (a) {kings} $\subset$ {black cards in a pack}
    (b) {multiples of 3} $\subset$ {multiples of 6}
    (c) {multiples of 6} $\subset$ {multiples of 3}

5   Consider the set $A = \{$ace of clubs, ace of hearts, ace of spades, ace of diamonds$\}$, which we will shorten to $A = \{c, h, s, d\}$. When we choose some cards from this set we are choosing a subset.
    (a) Write down a subset of A that has three members. Is your answer the only one? What are the others?
    (b) Now list the subsets of A that have two members.
    (c) List the subsets of A that have only one member.
    (d) All these subsets are called proper subsets of A. You should have listed a total of 14 (4+6+4).
        There are two other possible subsets. One is the subset which contains none of the cards. This will be considered in Chapter 4. Can you think of the other one?

Because each element of a set A belongs to A, we can write $A \subset A$. The set with no elements is also a subset of A. However, some people do not think these two subsets are 'proper' subsets of *A*. We define a *proper subset* as a subset of *A* that contains at least one member, but not all the members, of the set *A*.

6 List the proper subsets of these sets.
   (*a*) {red, orange, green}
   (*b*) {on, off}
   (*c*) {1}

Exercise B

This exercise will classify quadrilaterals according to their properties. A *convex quadrilateral* is one in which every interior angle is less than 180°. We shall use the following sets. (Figure 1 shows typical members from each set.)
Q = {convex quadrilaterals}, P = {parallelograms}, H = {rhombuses},
K = {kites}, R = {rectangles}, S = {squares}, T = {trapezia},
I = {isosceles trapezia}, A = {arrowheads}

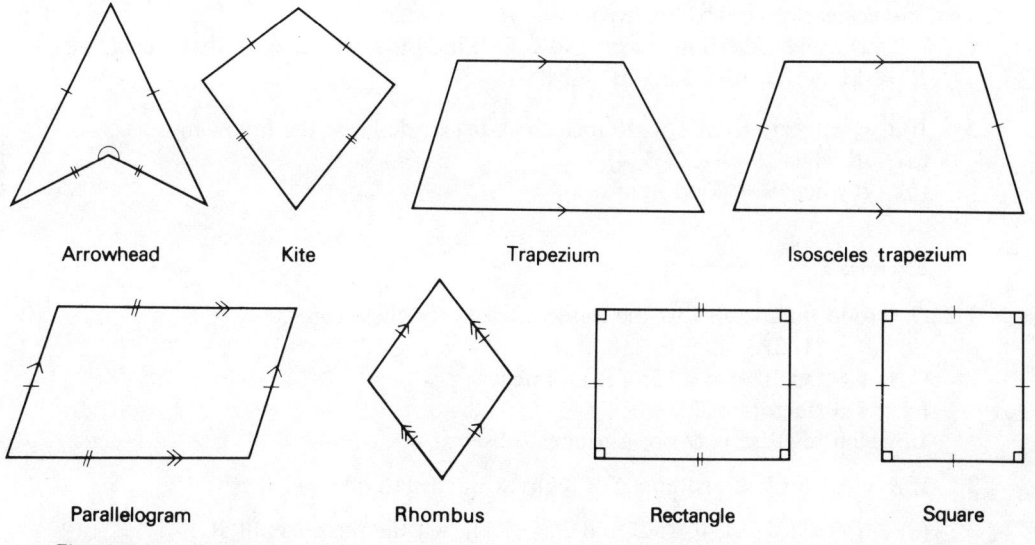

Figure 1

1 Which of the following are not subsets of Q? A, H, I, K, P, R, S, T

2 (*a*) Is $P \subset H$? (*b*) Is $H \subset P$?

3 List the proper subsets of (*a*) T, (*b*) H.

4 Which of these are true? Which are false?
   (*a*) $S \subset R$ (*b*) $T \not\subset T$ (*c*) $I \not\subset T$
   (*d*) $K \subset S$ (*e*) $K \not\subset H$ (*f*) $P \subset K$

1.3 The universal set

If $R = \{$king of hearts, king of diamonds$\}$, how many elements do not belong to R? As it stands, this is an impossible question to answer. We need some more information. Are we dealing with (a) just the four kings, (b) all the picture cards, or (c) a complete pack of 52 cards?

▷ 1 How many elements do not belong to R in each of the cases (a), (b) and (c)?

2 If 24 elements do not belong to R, suggest a set of which R is a subset.

The set of all possible elements that we want to consider in a particular situation is called the *universal set* for that situation. We use the symbol $\mathscr{E}$ to stand for this set.

Note that for any given set there are many possible universal sets. Which universal set is the most appropriate in a particular problem is usually determined by the problem. You must state clearly what you are taking as the universal set before you answer the problem.

The elements of $\mathscr{E}$ which are not members of a set R form a set called the *complement* of R, which is written as R'.

Thus if $\mathscr{E} = \{$the four kings$\}$ and $R = \{$king of hearts, king of diamonds$\}$, then $R' = \{$king of spades, king of clubs$\}$.

3 If $\mathscr{E} = \{$integers from 1 to 10 inclusive$\}$, list or describe the following sets.
 (a) A' when $A = \{1, 2, 3, 4\}$
 (b) B when $B' = \{$odd numbers$\}$

Exercise C

▷ 1 $O = \{$odd numbers$\}$. List the elements of O for these cases.
 (a) $\mathscr{E} = \{1, 2, 3, 4, 5, 6, 7, 8, 9, 10\}$
 (b) $\mathscr{E} = \{x: 10 < x < 15, x \text{ is an integer}\}$
 (c) $\mathscr{E} = \{$factors of 21$\}$
 In which of these is O not a proper subset of $\mathscr{E}$?

2 If $\mathscr{E} = \{$quadrilaterals$\}$ and $C = \{$convex quadrilaterals$\}$, what is C'?

3 (a) If $\mathscr{E} = \{-2, -1, 0, 1, 2\}$ and $P = \{1, 2\}$, list the members of P'.
 (b) What is the complement of P'? (That is the complement of the complement of P.)

4 List the members of $\mathscr{E}$, X and X' when $X = \{$numbers divisible by 2$\}$ and $\mathscr{E} = \{x: -4 < x < 4, x \text{ is an integer}\}$.

1.4 Venn diagrams

The relation between a set and its complement, and the elements contained in them, can be shown by means of a Venn diagram (named after John Venn, a British logician of the nineteenth century). Figure 2 shows how this is done.

We usually depict the universal set by a rectangle, and it is understood that all the elements of the universal set are enclosed within this rectangle. Subsets are shown by

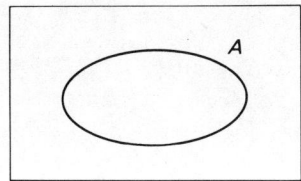

Figure 2

closed curves. Although the letter naming the set (*A* in Figure 2) might be written outside the curve, it is understood that the elements of *A* are inside the curve.

1 Copy Figure 2 and shade the part that represents A'.

If $\mathscr{E} = \{1, 2, 3, 4, 5, 6, 7, 8, 9\}$ and $A = \{$prime numbers$\}$, the diagram becomes as in Figure 3.

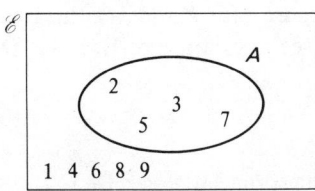

Figure 3

2 (*a*) If $R = \{10, 11, 12\}$ and $R' = \{$positive integers less than 10$\}$, what are the elements of $\mathscr{E}$?
(*b*) Draw a Venn diagram to show these sets.

Subsets in Venn diagrams

The Venn diagram of Figure 4 shows some of the subsets of Exercise B when $\mathscr{E} = \{$quadrilaterals$\}$.

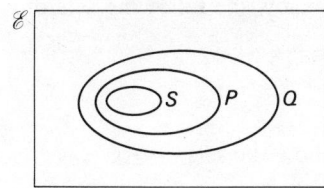

Figure 4

The case in which two sets have some elements in common can also be shown by a Venn diagram. For example, if
  $\mathscr{E} = \{$letters of the English alphabet$\}$,
  $V = \{a, e, i, o, u\}$,
and $M = \{$letters in the word *mathematical*$\}$,
then V and M 'overlap', as is shown in the Venn diagram of Figure 5 (overleaf).

7

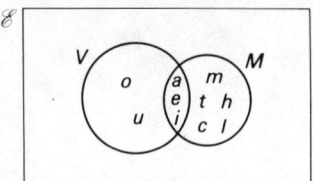

Figure 5

Note that when we draw Venn diagrams, we sometimes put down all the elements of the universal set (as in Figure 3), sometimes only some of the elements (Figure 5), and sometimes none of the individual elements (Figure 4). (Anyway, it would be impossible to list the individual elements of the sets shown in Figure 4 as each set contains an infinite number of elements.) The decision to show none, some or all of the individual elements on a Venn diagram is one that you have to make in the light of the particular situation or question.

Although it is neater to use circles for subsets (as in Figure 5 for V and M), this is not essential. Sometimes rectangles are more appropriate (see question **6** of Exercise D).

Exercise D

1 Draw Venn diagrams to illustrate (*a*) question **2**, (*b*) question **3** of Exercise C.

2 (*a*) Draw a Venn diagram to show $A = $ {letters in the word *mathematics*}, $B = $ {letters in the word *scheme*}, and $\mathscr{E} = $ {letters of the alphabet}.
   (*b*) What is the relation between A and B?

3 Draw a Venn diagram to show the sets $P = $ {prime numbers}, $E = $ {even numbers}, and $\mathscr{E} = \{n: 1 \leqslant n \leqslant 10, n \text{ is an integer}\}$.

4 Draw a Venn diagram for a universal set $\mathscr{E}$, and sets L and M when $L \subset M$. Shade L'.
   Are these true or false? (*a*) $M \subset L'$ (*b*) $L \subset M'$ (*c*) $L' \supset M'$

5 Draw two Venn diagrams with $\mathscr{E} = $ {quadrilaterals} to show the following sets of Exercise B.
   (*a*) I, T, P
   (*b*) P, R, H, S

6 If $\mathscr{E} = $ {counting numbers}, draw a Venn diagram to show the sets $E = $ {even numbers} and $O = $ {odd numbers}.

Summary

(1) The following symbols have been introduced.
     $\{\ \}, :, A = \{\ldots\}, \subset, \not\subset, \supset, \not\supset, \in, \notin, A', \mathscr{E}$.
(2) A Venn diagram shows the relation between sets and a universal set. (See Figure 6.)

8

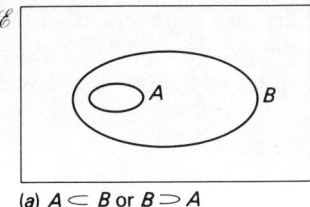

(a) $A \subset B$ or $B \supset A$

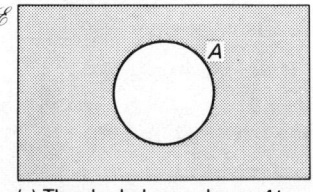

(b) $x \in P$ and $x \in Q$
    $y \in P$ but $y \notin Q$

(c) The shaded area shows A'

Figure 6

(3) A set is a collection of things. A set is denoted by a capital letter. An object belonging to a set is called a member or an element of that set. In Figure 6(b) x is a member of P (written $x \in P$).

(4) All the elements of a set are different. The order in which they are listed does not matter. If two sets have the same elements they are equal sets. A set should be well-defined – it must be possible to decide whether any particular object belongs to that set or not.

(5) A set may be defined in three ways:
  (a) by listing the elements of the set, as in $P = \{2, 3, 5, 7\}$,
  (b) by giving a description of the set, as in $P = \{$prime numbers less than 10$\}$,
  (c) by a formula or expression that can be used to determine whether or not an object belongs to the set, as in $P = \{x: x < 10, x$ is a prime number$\}$.

(6) When all the members of a set A also belong to a set B, then A is a subset of B (written $A \subset B$). Set B therefore contains all the elements of set A, and this can be written $B \supset A$. (See Figure 6(a).)
  A is a proper subset if it contains at least one, but not all, the elements of B.

(7) The universal set $\mathscr{E}$ for a given situation is the set containing all the elements we wish to consider in that situation. The complement A' of A contains all the elements of $\mathscr{E}$ that are not in A. (See Figure 6(c).)

Post-test

For this test, $L = \{$consonants in the English alphabet$\}$,
$M = \{$integers between 0 and 12$\}$, $N = \{$multiples of 3 or 5 between 0 and 16$\}$.

1 List the elements of L, M, and N.
2 A is the subset of L containing the first six elements of that set when written down in alphabetical order. Copy and complete the following, using the symbols $\in$, $\notin$, $\subset$, $\not\subset$ where necessary.
  (a) $A = \{\quad\}$ (b) $A \,\square\, L$ (c) $a \,\square\, A$
  (d) $g \,\square\, A$ and $g \,\square\, L$ (e) $t \,\square\, A$ and $t \,\square\, L$ (f) $L \,\square\, A$

3   B is the set that contains all those elements of M that are also members of N. List the elements of B, and draw a Venn diagram to show the elements of the sets M, N and B. Of the possible universal sets for this question, describe the one that has the smallest number of elements.

Assignment

1   Give two alternative definitions of $A = \{x: {}^-2 \leqslant x \leqslant 2, x \text{ is an integer}\}$.

2   $\mathscr{E} = \{\text{positive even integers}\}$, $P = \{\text{multiples of 5}\}$, and $Q = \{38, 40, 42, 44\}$.
    (a) List the members of P.
    (b) Draw a Venn diagram to show the connection between P, Q and $\mathscr{E}$.
    (c) What is x if $x \in P$ and $x \in Q$?
    (d) What is x if $x \in P'$ and $x \in Q$?

3   Insert the correct symbol (from $\in$, $\notin$, $\subset$, $\not\subset$) between the following pairs.
    (a) $\{3\}$ {counting numbers}   (b) 3 {counting numbers}
    (c) 3 {even numbers}   (d) $\{3\}$ {even numbers}
    (e) $\{3, 6\}$ {counting numbers}   (f) $\{3, 6\}$ {even numbers}

4   Can you find a set X, a universal set $\mathscr{E}$, and an element a such that $a \in X$ and $a \in X'$?

5   Define three sets A, B and C such that $A \subset B$ and $B \subset C$. Is A a subset of C? Draw a Venn diagram to show A, B and C.

6   A, B and C are any three sets such that $A \subset B$ and $B \subset C$. Say whether each of the following is always true, sometimes true or never true.
    (a) $A \subset C$ (b) $A' \supset C'$ (c) $C \subset A'$

7   $P = \{x: {}^-1 \leqslant x \leqslant 7\}$, $Q = \{x: 4x - 7 = {}^-11\}$, $R = \{x: x < 2\}$, and $\mathscr{E} = \{\text{integers}\}$.
    (a) What is x if $x \in P$ and $x \in R$?
    (b) What is x if $x \in P$ and $x \notin R$?
    (c) What is x if $x \in P$, $x \in Q$, and $x \in R$?
    (d) Is it true that $R \subset P$?
    (e) Is it true that $Q \subset P$?

8   State whether the following are true or false. If they are false, give a counter-example.
    (a) {quadrilaterals with 1 line of symmetry} $\subset$ {trapezia}
    (b) {quadrilaterals with 2 lines of symmetry} $\subset$ {quadrilaterals with 4 equal sides}
    (c) {quadrilaterals with rotational symmetry of order 2} $\subset$ {quadrilaterals with opposite sides parallel}

BOURNEMOUTH SCHOOL FOR GIRLS
LIBRARY

Answers

Pre-test

1. (a) A prime number is an integer greater than 1 that is divisible only by 1 and the integer itself.
   (b) 2, 3, 5, 7, 11, 13, 17, 19, 23, 29
   (Note that 1 is not a prime number.)
2. A possible answer is 3, 6, 9, 12, 15, 18. A multiple of 3 is a number that is divisible by 3 (3 goes into it exactly).
3. (a) A quadrilateral is a flat, four-sided figure with straight edges.
   (b) Some quadrilaterals are arrowhead, kite, trapezium, isosceles trapezium, parallelogram, rhombus, rectangle, square.
4. x is a number that is greater than 0, but less than or equal to 8. (So x is a positive number less than or equal to 8.)

1.1 Set notation

1. See the answer to pre-test question 3(b) for some elements of set (b). The elements of set (c) are a, c, e, h, i, l, m, t.
2. Set (a) contains 9 elements. Set (b) contains an infinite number of elements.
3. Set (a) is {11, 12, 13, 14, 15, 16, 17, 18, 19}. The numbers do not have to be in this order.
4. (a) 'The set of tall people' is not well-defined because we have not stated the minimum height for a person to be considered as 'tall'.
   (b) Set (b) is well-defined. Although it has an infinite number of members, it is possible to state definitely whether any particular shape is a quadrilateral or not.
5. $A = \{2, 4, 6, 8, 10\}$
   $B = \{\text{red, orange, yellow, green, blue, indigo, violet}\}$
6. (a) $10 \in A$ (b) $10 \notin S$ (c) $15 \in S$ (d) $12 \notin A$
7. $C = \{2, 4, 6, 8, \ldots, 498\}$
   $D = \{5, 10, 15, 20, \ldots\}$
   In both cases you can include more elements if you want to make the pattern clearer, but it is not wise to list fewer than three elements before the dots.
8. $E = \{\text{square numbers}\}$
   $F = \{\text{odd numbers between 100 and 200}\}$
9. $Z = \{\ldots, {}^-2, {}^-1, 0, 1, 2, 3, \ldots\}$

Exercise A

1. (a) {3, 6, 9, 12, 15, 18}
   (b) {sight, touch, taste, smell, hearing}
   (c) {2}
   (d) {101, 102, 103, 104, ...}
   (e) {1, 2, 3, 4, 5, 6, 7, 8}

2   (a) {vowels}
    (b) {odd integers greater than 0} or {positive odd integers}
    (c) {the four suits in a pack of cards}
    (d) {prime numbers less than 20} or {the first eight prime numbers}
    (e) {even integers} or {even integers including 0}

3   $A = \{1, 3, 5, 7, 9\}$
    $B = \{1, 4, 9, 16, 25, \ldots\}$
    $C = \{7, 8, 9, 10, 11, 12, 13, 14, 15, 16\}$
    (a) $x = 1$ or 9 (b) $x = 9$ or 16 (c) $x = 9$
    (d) $x = 1, 3$ or 5 (e) $x = 8, 10, 11, 12, 13, 14$ or 15

4   (a) $169 \in \{$square numbers$\}$
    (b) $d \notin \{$vowels$\}$
    (c) $6 \in \{x: 2 < x < 22, x$ is an even integer$\}$

5   (a) is not well-defined. How far from the coast is 'off Tobago'?
    (b) is not well-defined. We have not defined 'sunny' precisely.
    (c) is well-defined.

1.2 Subsets

1   (a) $A = \{1, 2, 4, 8, 16\}$
        $B = \{1, 2, 3, 4, 6, 8, 12, 16, 24, 48\}$
    (b) All the elements of A are also elements of B.

2   B is not a subset of A. 3, 6, 12, 24 and 48 are members of B but not of A.

3   If $P \subset Q$ and $Q \supset P$, then P and Q must both contain the same elements. So $P = Q$.

4   (a) is false, as the kings of hearts and diamonds are not black cards.
    (b) is false, as 3, 9, 15, … are multiples of 3 but not of 6.
    (c) is true.

5   (a) $\{c, h, s\}, \{c, h, d\}, \{c, s, d\}, \{h, s, d\}$
    (b) $\{c, h\}, \{c, s\}, \{c, d\}, \{h, s\}, \{h, d\}, \{s, d\}$
    (c) $\{c\}, \{h\}, \{s\}, \{d\}$
    (d) The set $\{c, h, s, d\}$ is also a subset.

6   (a) $\{r, o\}, \{r, g\}, \{o, g\}, \{r\}, \{o\}, \{g\}$ (where $r =$ red, $o =$ orange and $g =$ green)
    (b) {on}, {off}
    (c) There are no proper subsets of a set that has only one member.

Exercise B

1   A is not a subset of Q. All the others are.

2   (a) No (b) Yes
    All rhombuses are special cases of parallelograms, therefore $H \subset P$. However, there are many parallelograms that are not rhombuses, hence $P \not\subset H$.

3   (a) I, P, R, S and H are all proper subsets of T.
    (b) S is the only proper subset of H.

4   (a) True (b) False (c) False (d) False
    (e) True (f) False
    Rhombuses and squares are special cases of kites, hence $H \subset K$ and $S \subset K$. Not all kites are rhombuses, hence $K \not\subset H$. Not all kites are squares, hence $K \not\subset S$.

1.3 The universal set

1 (a) 2 (b) 10 (c) 50
2 {red cards}
3 (a) $A' = \{5, 6, 7, 8, 9, 10\}$ = {integers from 5 to 10 inclusive}
   (b) $B = \{2, 4, 6, 8, 10\}$ = {even numbers}

Exercise C

1 (a) $O = \{1, 3, 5, 7, 9\}$
   (b) $\mathscr{E} = \{11, 12, 13, 14\}$, so $O = \{11, 13\}$
   (c) $\mathscr{E} = \{1, 3, 7, 21\}$, so $O = \{1, 3, 7, 21\}$
   O is not a proper subset in part (c) as it contains all the elements of $\mathscr{E}$.
2 C' = {non-convex quadrilaterals}
   = {quadrilaterals with a reflex or re-entrant angle}
   An arrowhead is one type of non-convex quadrilateral.
3 (a) $P' = \{^-2, ^-1, 0\}$
   (b) $(P')' = \{1, 2\} = P$
4 $\mathscr{E} = \{^-3, ^-2, ^-1, 0, 1, 2, 3\}$, $X = \{^-2, 0, 2\}$, $X' = \{^-3, ^-1, 1, 3\}$

1.4 Venn diagrams

1 The shaded area of Figure A represents A'.

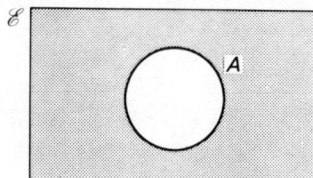

Figure A

2 (a) $\mathscr{E}$ = {positive integers less than 13} = $\{1, 2, 3, 4, \ldots, 12\}$
   (b) See Figure B.

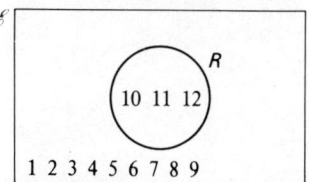

Figure B

Exercise D

1   See Figure C. As we have included the elements in the diagram for (b), it is not essential to define the sets underneath.

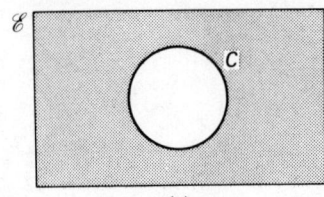 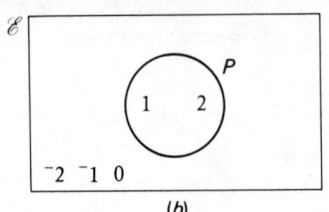

$\mathscr{E} = \{\text{quadrilaterals}\}$

$C = \{\text{convex quadrilaterals}\}$

C' is shaded

Figure C

2   (a)   See Figure D.
    (b) $B \subset A$ (or $A \supset B$)

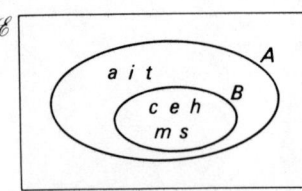

$\mathscr{E} = \{\text{letters of the alphabet}\}$
Figure D

3   See Figure E.

Figure E

4   See Figure F.
    (a) False   (b) False   (c) True

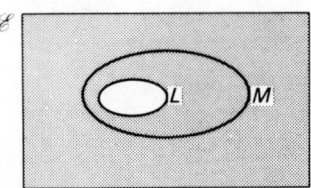

L' is shaded
Figure F

14

5 See Figure G.

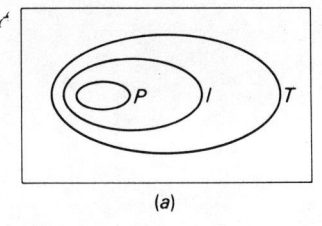
(a)

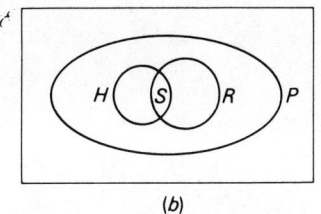
(b)

Figure G

6 In this example, E and O contain all the elements of $\mathscr{E}$ between them, but no element belongs to both E and O. Hence $O = E'$ and $E = O'$. Figure H shows some possible Venn diagrams.

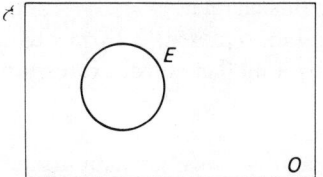
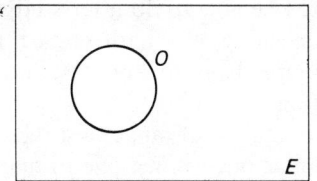
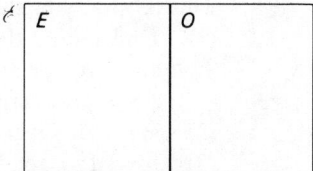

Figure H

Post-test

1 $L = \{b, c, d, f, g, h, j, k, l, m, n, p, q, r, s, t, v, w, x, y, z\}$
$M = \{1, 2, 3, 4, 5, 6, 7, 8, 9, 10, 11\}$
$N = \{3, 5, 6, 9, 10, 12, 15\}$

2 (a) $A = \{b, c, d, f, g, h\}$ (b) $A \subset L$ (c) $a \notin A$
(d) $g \in A$ and $g \in L$ (e) $t \notin A$ and $t \in L$ (f) $L \not\subset A$

3 $B = \{3, 5, 6, 9, 10\}$
See Figure I.

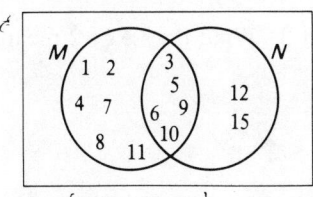

$B = \{3, 5, 6, 9, 10\}$

Figure I

The smallest possible $\mathscr{E}$ is such that all its elements are members of M and/or N.
$\mathscr{E} = \{1, 2, 3, 4, 5, 6, 7, 8, 9, 10, 11, 12, 15\}$
= {integers between 0 and 16, excluding 13 and 14}

2 Relations

Objectives

This is what you should be able to do after studying this chapter.
(1) Understand the meaning of a mathematical relation, represent it by means of an arrow or mapping diagram, and describe it by a mathematical expression or a verbal description.
(2) Write down the domain and range of a relation.
(3) Identify a relation as one-to-one, one-to-many, many-to-one or many-to-many.
(4) Identify the inverse of a relation, and recognise when a relation is self-inverse.

Pre-test

1 $2^2 = 2 \times 2 = 4$. Write the meaning and value of each of the following in a similar way.
   (a) 3^2 (b) $^-4^2 (=(^-4)^2)$ (c) $(\tfrac{1}{2})^2$
   (d) $2^3 (=2 \times 2 \times 2)$ (e) $^-2^3$ (f) $(\tfrac{3}{4})^3$

2 (a) $2x$ means 'multiply x by 2'. What does $5x$ mean?
   Write the value of $5x$ for each of the following.
   (b) $x = 3$ (c) $x = {}^-2$ (d) $x = \tfrac{1}{3}$

3 (a) $2x-3$ means 'multiply x by 2, and then subtract 3'. What does $5x+2$ mean?
   Write the value of $5x+2$ for each of the following.
   (b) $x = 3$ (c) $x = {}^-2$ (d) $x = \tfrac{1}{3}$

4 (a) What does $5/x \left(\text{or } \dfrac{5}{x}\right)$ mean?
   Write the value of $5/x$ for each of the following.
   (b) $x = 10$ (c) $x = {}^-2$ (d) $x = \tfrac{1}{4}$

5 (a) List the members of the set {prime numbers less than 20}.
   (b) List the factors of 12. Which of these are prime numbers? These are the *prime factors* of 12.

6 List the prime factors of the following.
   (a) 8 (b) 18 (c) 35

2.1 Mapping machines

You may already have met the idea of a 'machine' that can carry out the operations of addition, subtraction, multiplication and division on numbers. For example, in Figure 1 the rectangular box represents a 'multiply by 3' machine. Machines like these are called *mapping machines*.

Figure 1

The number that we put into a machine is called the input, or *object*. The number that comes out is the output, or *image*. In Figure 1, the object is 5 and the image is 15. We say that 5 *is mapped onto* 15.

1 (a) 2 is put into a 'multiply by 3' machine. What is the output?
(b) What is the image of 4?
(c) What is 3 mapped onto by this machine?

We can show the effect of the 'multiply by 3' machine by a *mapping diagram*, as in Figure 2. We read this as '1 is mapped onto 3, 2 onto 6' and so on. The arrow stands for 'is mapped onto', so we can say that this diagram shows the mapping $x \to 3x$.

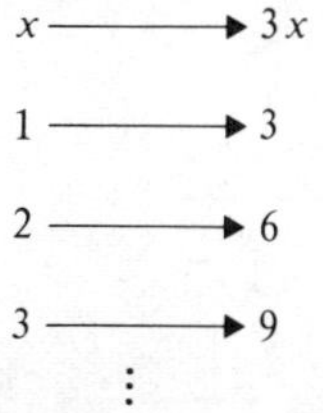

$x \longrightarrow 3x$

$1 \longrightarrow 3$

$2 \longrightarrow 6$

$3 \longrightarrow 9$

⋮

Figure 2

The set of numbers on the left $\{1, 2, 3, \ldots\}$ is called the *object set*, or *domain*. That on the right $\{3, 6, 9, \ldots\}$ is called the *image set*, or *range*. In this chapter we shall nearly always use a small set of three or four members as the domain. However, the domain and range can often be much larger, and frequently are infinite in size as, for example, when they are the set of all real numbers.

2 Copy and complete the following mapping diagrams.
(a) $x \to x-2$ (b) $x \to x+7$ (c) $x \to \square$
   $1 \to \square$ $\square \to 10$ $1 \to \frac{1}{2}$
   $2 \to \square$ $\square \to 13$ $2 \to 1$
   $3 \to \square$ $\square \to 16$ $3 \to 1\frac{1}{2}$
   $4 \to \square$ $\square \to 20$ $4 \to \square$

Two other ways of drawing mapping diagrams are shown in Figure 3 (overleaf).

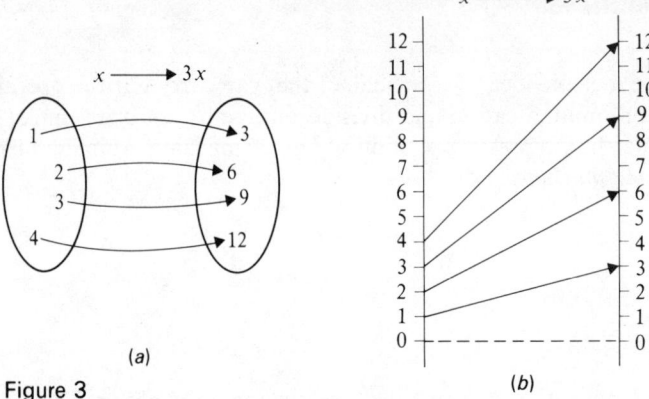

Figure 3

In Figure 3(b) we use number lines to represent the domain and range. This idea is especially useful when the domain consists of all the real numbers. The arrows then show only a selection of the possible mappings. The effect of a mapping is shown more clearly if the same scale can be used for both domain and range.

2.2 Relations

Figure 4 shows a family tree, from which we can write down relationships existing between various members of the family. For example, Janet is Martin's cousin, Peter is Elsie's son, Judith and Janet are both granddaughters of Mary and Tom. (We shall be referring to Figure 4 quite often in this chapter, so you may find it helpful to copy it onto a separate piece of paper.)

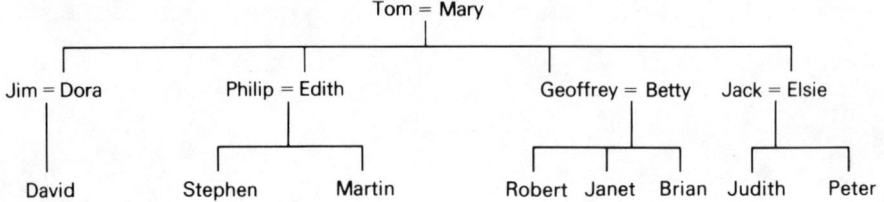

Figure 4

▷ 1 What relationship is shown by the ' = ' sign?

There are many relationships (or *relations*) we can extract from this tree. Figure 5 shows an example of the relation 'is the brother of' on the set of children of Tom and Mary. In this diagram, the arrow represents the statement 'is the brother of'. So Geoffrey → Elsie is read as 'Geoffrey is the brother of Elsie'. Diagrams like Figure 5 are called *arrow diagrams*.

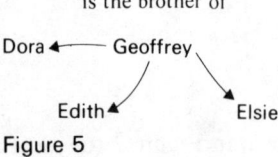

Figure 5

2 Draw an arrow diagram to represent the relation 'is the sister of' for the same four people.

Of course, the relation 'is a sister of' can still be shown by a mapping diagram as in Figure 6, with the domain and range listed separately.

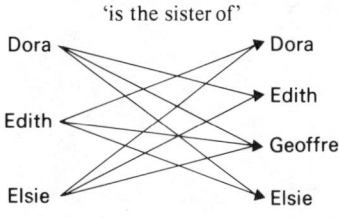

Figure 6

3 (a) Draw a mapping diagram for the relation 'is the uncle of' for the domain {Philip, Geoffrey}.
(b) What are the images of Geoffrey?

Arrow and mapping diagrams can be used to illustrate other types of relations. Mathematically, a *relation* is any connection between the members of two sets, or amongst the members of one set. Mappings such as $x \to 3x$ are examples of relations. So another name for a mapping diagram is a *relation diagram*.

The connection can be given as a *verbal description* (such as 'is the sister of', 'has as a brother', 'is a factor of', 'is one-third of') or as a *mathematical expression* (such as $x \to 3x$, 'multiply by 3').

In a verbal description, the object is described in terms of the image. For example, for Dora → Geoffrey, 'Dora is the sister of Geoffrey' describes Dora in terms of Geoffrey.

4 (a) Copy and complete the diagram below for the relation 'is a factor of'.

```
'is a factor of'
    2        5
    3        6
    5        7
    7        8
             9
             10
```

(b) What is the image of 7?
(c) Of which number or numbers is 6 an image?

Exercise A

1 Draw an arrow diagram for the relation 'is a cousin of' on the set {David, Stephen, Martin, Judith, Peter} from Figure 4.

2 Draw the mapping diagram for the relation 'is a granddaughter of' for the members of the family shown in Figure 4.

3 From Figure 4 draw the mapping diagram to show the number of children of Dora, Edith, Betty and Elsie.

4 Draw an arrow diagram for the relation 'is a factor of' on the set {2, 3, 4, 6}.

5 (a) Copy and complete this mapping diagram for the relation 'is less than'.
   'is less than'
   3   13
   7   17
   18   18
   19   20
   (b) What are the images of 7?
   (c) Of which numbers is 18 an image?
   (d) The image of the set {18, 19} is the set {20}. What is the image of the set {7, 18}?

2.3 Mappings

In a verbal description of a relation (for example, 'x is the sister of y'), the object x is described in terms of the image y. Consider the mapping
   $x \to y$
   $2 \to 8$
   $4 \to 16$
   $6 \to 24$
   $8 \to 32$
Here, 2 is a quarter of 8, 6 is a quarter of 24, and so on.

1 What is the verbal description of this relation?

Verbal descriptions are used when we describe an object in terms of its image. However, we often want to show how an image is obtained from its object.

2 In this mapping, what must we do to x to obtain its image?

We call this method of describing a relation the *mathematical expression*. In a mathematical expression, the image is given in terms of its object. The mathematical expression for the above relation is 'multiply by 4' or $x \to 4x$.

So we have two ways of describing a relation.
(1) Verbal description. This gives the object in terms of image, as in x is a quarter of y.
(2) Mathematical expression. This tells us what has to be done to the object to obtain the image, as in 'multiply by 4' or $x \to 4x$. (x has to be multiplied by 4 to obtain the image y.)

Exercise B

1. (a) Copy and complete this relation diagram.
$$x \to$$
$$-3 \to$$
$$-2 \to 2$$
$$-1 \to 3$$
$$0 \to$$
$$1 \to 5$$
   (b) What is the verbal description of this mapping?
   (c) What is 1 mapped onto?
   (d) What is the image of -2?
   (e) What is mapped onto 1?
   (f) What is the object of 4?

2. Repeat question **1** for this mapping diagram.
$$x \to x^2$$
   2   4
   1   1
   0   0
   -1
   -2

3. Write down the images of (i) 7, (ii) $\frac{1}{2}$, (iii) -2, for these mappings.
   (a) $x \to 3x$ (b) $x \to x - 2$
   (c) $x \to x/2$ (d) $x \to 12 - x$

4. What is the range of the mapping $x \to 2x - 1$ for these domains?
   (a) $\{1, 2, 3, 4\}$ (b) $\{-2, -1, 0, 1, 2\}$ (c) {all integers}

2.4 Different types of relations

Look at the two mapping diagrams that you completed for questions **1** and **2**, Exercise B. Each has its own 'pattern' of arrows. Consider the following relations on a set of three people.

1. Which of the diagrams in Figure 7 do you think has the same kind of arrow pattern as (a) question **1**, (b) question **2** of Exercise B?

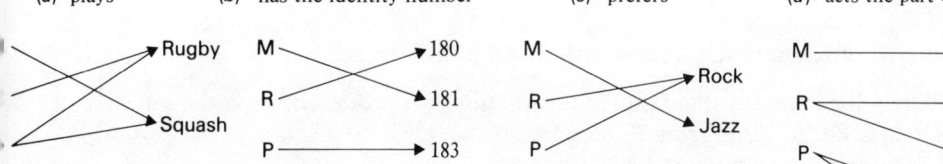

(a) 'plays'   (b) 'has the identity number'   (c) 'prefers'   (d) 'acts the part of'

Figure 7

In Figure 7(a), there is at least one sport with more than one arrow coming to it, and at least one person from whom more than one arrow comes. We say that the relation is *many-to-many*. In Figure 7(b), no person has more than one number, and each number is connected to one person only. This is a *one-to-one* relation.

Figures 7(c) and 7(d) need to be looked at more carefully. Figure 7(c) shows a *many-to-one* relation. More than one person may prefer a particular type of music, but a particular individual can prefer only one type of music. Figure 7(d), however, shows a *one-to-many* relation. One actor may play many parts, but each part is played by one actor only.

2 (a) Copy and complete this mapping diagram for the family whose tree is shown in Figure 4.

'is the brother of'
Robert   Robert
Brian   Janet
            Brian

(b) What type of relation does this illustrate?

3 The many-to-one and one-to-many relations can be confusing. Look carefully at Figure 7 again, and then copy and complete the mapping diagrams below. Write under each diagram the type of relation it shows.

(a) x → number of prime factors of x

3
6
16
30

(b) x → 12/x

1
2
3
4
6

(c) 'is greater than'

⁻2   ⁻3
⁻1   ⁻1
0   1
1
2

(d) 'is divisible by'

7   2
9   3
10   5
        7

Exercise C

1 What type of relations are questions 1, 2 and 3 of Exercise A?

2 (a) Draw the mapping diagram for the relation x → brother of x on the set {Dora, Edith, Elsie} from Figure 4.
(b) What type of relation is this?

3 From Figure 4 select a relation that is a one-to-one correspondence. What do you notice about the number of members of the domain, and the number of members of the range? Is this true for all the one-to-one relations that we have met so far? Is this true for the other types of relations?

4 Copy and complete the following diagrams. Write underneath each diagram the type of relation it shows.

(a) $x \to$ largest prime factor of x
12
21
35
64

(b) $x \to x^3$
$^-2$
$^-1$
0
1
2

(c) 'is divisible by'
2          $\frac{1}{5}$
$2\frac{1}{2}$ $\frac{1}{4}$
$3\frac{1}{3}$ $\frac{1}{3}$
$4\frac{1}{4}$

(d) $x \to$ number of letters in x
One
Two
Three
Four
Five

2.5 Inverse relations

What happens if we reverse the arrows in this mapping?

'is the granddaughter of'

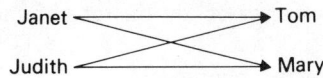

Figure 8

1 (a) Show the effect of reversing the arrows by completing the diagram below. Note that {Tom, Mary} is now the domain.

'is a ... of'
Tom   Janet
Mary   Judith

(b) What relation does this new diagram represent?

Let us now reverse the arrows of the mapping $x \to 2x$ over the domain $\{^-2, ^-1, 0, 1, 2\}$. This time we combine the two diagrams.

Original
$x \to 2x$
$2 \to 4$
$1 \to 2$
$0 \to 0$
$^-1 \to ^-2$
$^-2 \to ^-4$

Reversed
$4 \to 2$
$2 \to 1$
$0 \to 0$
$^-2 \to ^-1$
$^-4 \to ^-2$
$x \to \frac{1}{2}x$

Notice that the reversed diagram reverses the effect of the original. For instance, $^{-}1$ is mapped onto $^{-}2$ by $x \to 2x$, and then $x \to \tfrac{1}{2}x$ maps $^{-}2$ back onto $^{-}1$. You should see that this happens for every number of the original domain. We say that $x \to \tfrac{1}{2}x$ is the *inverse mapping* of $x \to 2x$.

2 What is the inverse mapping of $x \to \tfrac{1}{2}x$?

We say that $x \to 2x$ and $x \to \tfrac{1}{2}x$ are *inverse mappings*. Each reverses the effect of the other. Similarly, for suitable domains, 'is the granddaughter of' and 'is the grandparent of' are inverse mappings or relations.

Consider the effect of applying the mapping $x \to x+3$ to any number, say 5. The result is $5+3 = 8$. Now apply the mapping $x \to x-3$ to this answer. We obtain $8-3 = 5$, the original number.

3 (a) Would we obtain the same result (that is, the number with which we started) no matter which number we took from the domain?
(b) What is the inverse of $x \to x+3$?
(c) What is the inverse of $x \to x-3$?
(d) What single mapping is equivalent to $x \to x+3$ followed by $x \to x-3$?

4 (a) What is the inverse of $x \to x/5$?
(b) Write down the single relation that is equivalent to $x \to x/5$ followed by its inverse.

5 Figure 9(a) shows the relation 'has a greatest prime factor of' on the set of numbers {12, 15, 18, 21}.
(a) Copy and complete Figure 9(b) to show the inverse relation.
(b) State the inverse relation in words.
(c) What kind of relation is 'has a greatest prime factor of'?

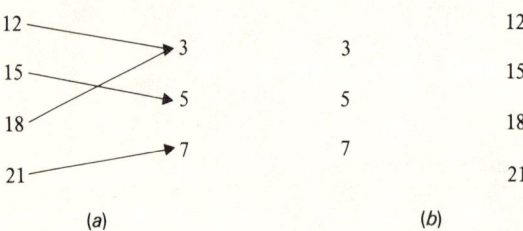

Figure 9

6 (a) Draw an arrow diagram to show the relation 'is a cousin of' on the set {David, Stephen, Martin} from Figure 4.
(b) Draw the diagram to show the inverse relation beside it.
(c) What do you notice about the two diagrams?

Relations of this kind, where the original relation and its inverse are identical, are called *self-inverse*.

7 (a) Copy and complete the mapping diagram below, and the diagram for the inverse.

$$x \longrightarrow 5-x$$

```
0 ———→ 5 ———→ 0
1           1
2           2
3           3
4           4
5           5
```
$$x \longrightarrow$$

(b) Is the mapping self-inverse?

Exercise D

1 Complete the table below for these relations and domains.
(a) $x \to x+4$, domain $\{6, 7, 8, 9\}$
(b) $x \to x^2$, domain $\{-1, -\frac{1}{2}, 0, \frac{1}{2}, 1\}$
(c) $x \to$ next largest integer, domain $\{\frac{1}{2}, 1, 1\frac{1}{2}, 2\}$
(d) $x \to 6/x$, domain $\{1, 1\frac{1}{2}, 2, 3, 4, 6\}$
(e) $x \to 15x$, domain $\{-4, -3, -2, -1, 0\}$

Relation	Type	Inverse	Type	Self-inverse?
(a)	One-to-one	$x \to x-4$	One-to-one	No
(b)				
(c)				
(d)				
(e)				

2 Complete a similar table for these relations and domains. (See Figure 4.)
(a) $x \to$ niece of x, domain {Jim, Philip, Geoffrey, Jack}
(b) $x \to$ brother of x, domain {Stephen, Martin, Robert, Brian}
(c) $x \to$ brother of x, domain {Robert, Brian, Janet}
(d) $x \to$ brother of x, domain {Janet, Judith}

Summary

(1) A relation is a connection, or mapping, between the members of two sets, or amongst the members of the same set.

(2) A relation can be shown by an arrow diagram (Figure 10(a)) or a mapping diagram (Figure 10(b)). A relation can be written as a verbal description (giving the object in terms of its image), as in
   'is the brother of' or 'is 2 less than',
or as a mathematical expression (giving the image in terms of the object), as in
   $x \to x+2$ or 'add 2'.

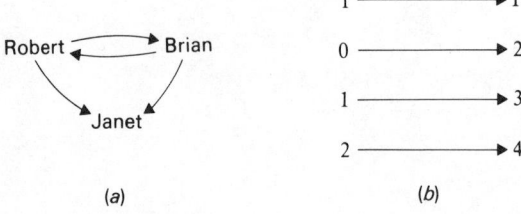

(a)   (b)

Figure 10

(3) The set with which we start is called the object set, or domain. The set with which we end is the image set, or range. A mapping links (or connects or maps) the members of the domain onto the members of the range. In short, the domain is mapped onto the range. In describing a mapping, we must state what the domain is.

(4) If the arrows are reversed in a mapping diagram, the new diagram represents the inverse relation. The inverse relations of the examples used in Figure 10 are (a) 'has as a brother' or $x \to$ brother of x, and (b) $x \to x-2$ or 'subtract 2'.

(5) There are four different types of relation. Figure 11 shows them.

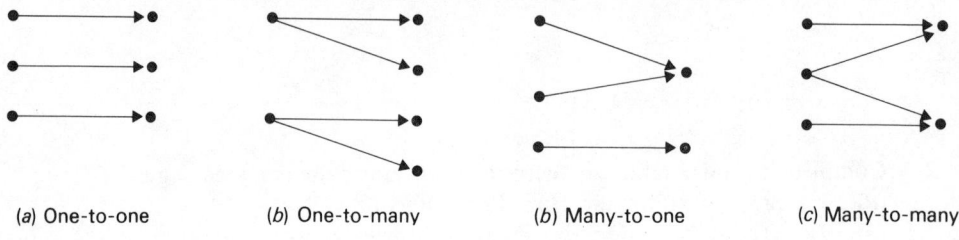

(a) One-to-one   (b) One-to-many   (b) Many-to-one   (c) Many-to-many

Figure 11

(6) In a self-inverse relation, the inverse relation is the same as the original relation.

Post-test

1 A machine maps n onto $3n-2$.
   (a) Draw a mapping diagram with domain {0, 3, 4, 6, 8}.
   (b) What is the image of 3?   (c) What is the image of 8?
   (d) Another number is added to the domain. The new number's image is 13. What is the new number?
   (e) What type of relation is this?   (f) List the elements of the range.
   (g) Write down the domain and the range for the inverse relation, and describe the inverse relation in the form $n \to \ldots$

2 For the following relations state what type they are, and whether or not they are self-inverse.
   (a) $x \to x^2+1$, domain $\{^-1, 0, 1, 2\}$
   (b) $x \to 8-x$, domain $\{0, 2, 4, 6, 8\}$
   (c) $x \to 8-x$, domain $\{0, 1, 2, 3, 4\}$
   (d) $x \to 8-x$, domain {real numbers}
   (e) $x \to$ cousin of x, domain {David, Judith, Peter} (See Figure 4.)

3 (a) Express the relation 'multiply by $\frac{1}{4}$' in two other ways.
   (b) Express the relation 'is a quarter of' in two other ways.
   (c) Are the relations (a) and (b) the same? If they are not, in what way are they connected?

Assignment

1 (a) Draw the mapping diagram for the relation $x \to 5x+2$ for the domain $\{^-2, ^-1, 0, 1, 2\}$.
   (b) Draw the mapping diagram for the inverse.

2 Choose a suitable domain from the members of the family shown in Figure 4 so that the relation '$x \to$ son of x' is many-to-one, and draw the mapping diagram.
   For questions 3 to 11, do the following.
   (a) List the image set.
   (b) State the type of relation.
   (c) State the type of the inverse relation.
   (d) State whether it is self-inverse or not.

3 $x \to$ greatest prime factor of x, domain $\{10, 60, 110, 160\}$
4 $x \to 3+2x$, domain $\{^-1, 0, 1, 2\}$
5 $x \to$ largest integer not greater than x, domain $\{0, \frac{1}{2}, 1, 1\frac{1}{2}, 2\}$
6 $x \to$ parent of x, domain {Robert, Janet, Brian} (See Figure 4.)
7 $x \to$ parent of x, domain {David} (See Figure 4.)
8 $x \to 12/x$, domain {real numbers except 0} (Why do we omit 0 from the domain?)
9 $x \to 10+x$, domain {real numbers}
10 $x \to 10-x$, domain {real numbers}
11 $x \to$ number of cars owned by x, domain {people living in Jersey}

12 Use Figure 4 to distinguish between the mappings 'is the sister of', 'has as a sister', and $x \to$ sister of x. What is the connection between these three relations?

Answers

Pre-test

1 (a) $3 \times 3 = 9$ (b) $^-4 \times ^-4 = 16$ (c) $\frac{1}{2} \times \frac{1}{2} = \frac{1}{4}$
   (d) $2 \times 2 \times 2 = 8$ (e) $^-2 \times ^-2 \times ^-2 = ^-8$ (f) $\frac{3}{4} \times \frac{3}{4} \times \frac{3}{4} = \frac{27}{64}$
2 (a) $5x$ means 'multiply x by 5'.
   (b) 15 (c) $^-10$ (d) $1\frac{2}{3}$

27

3 (a) $5x+2$ means 'multiply x by 5, and then add 2'.
  (b) 17 (c) $^-8$ (d) $3\frac{2}{3}$
4 (a) $5/x$ means 'divide 5 by x'.
  (b) $\frac{1}{2}$ (c) $^-2\frac{1}{2}$ (d) 20
5 (a) {2, 3, 5, 7, 11, 13, 17, 19}
  (b) 1, 2, 3, 4, 6, 12 are the factors of 12. The prime factors of 12 are 2 and 3.
6 (a) 2 (b) 2, 3 (c) 5, 7

2.1 Mapping machines

1 (a) 6 (b) 12 (c) 9

2 (a) $x \to x-2$ (b) $x \to x+7$ (c) $x \to \frac{1}{2}x$
      $1 \to ^-1$ $3 \to 10$ $1 \to \frac{1}{2}$
      $2 \to 0$ $6 \to 13$ $2 \to 1$
      $3 \to 1$ $9 \to 16$ $3 \to 1\frac{1}{2}$
      $4 \to 2$ $13 \to 20$ $4 \to 2$

2.2 Relations

1 The '=' sign represents 'is married to'.
2 See Figure A.

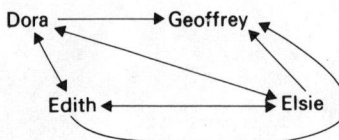

Figure A

3 (a) See Figure B.   (b) David, Stephen, Martin, Judith, Peter

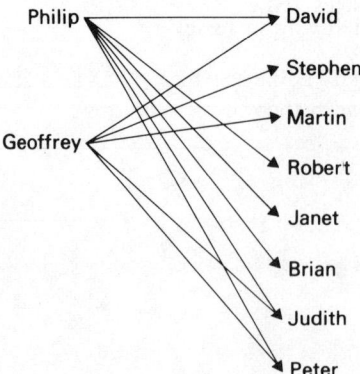

Figure B

28

4 (*a*) See Figure C. (*b*) 7 (*c*) 2, 3

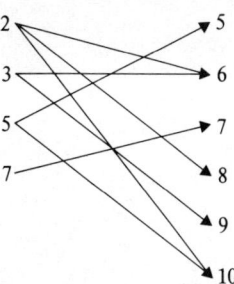

Figure C

Exercise A

1 See Figure D.
2 See Figure E.

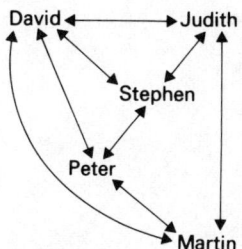

Figure D

Figure E

3 See Figure F.
4 See Figure G.

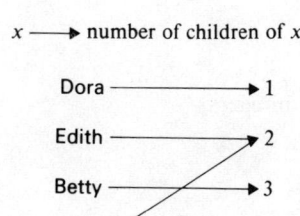

Figure F

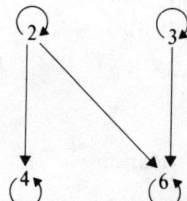

Figure G

5 (a) See Figure H. (b) 13, 17, 18, 20 (c) 3, 7
   (d) {13, 17, 18, 20}

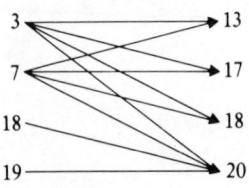

Figure H

2.3 Mappings

1 x is a quarter of y.

2 To obtain the image of x, x must be multiplied by 4.

Exercise B

1 (a) See Figure I. (b) x is 4 less than y.
   (c) 5 (d) 2 (e) ⁻3 (f) 0

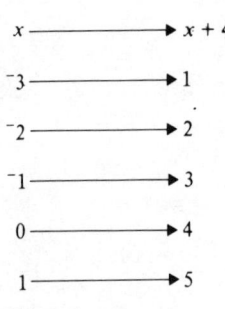 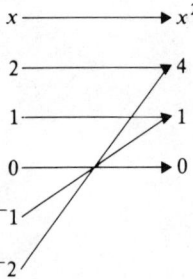

Figure I   Figure J

2 (a) See Figure J. (b) x is the square root of y.
   (c) 1 (d) 4 (e) ⁻1 and 1 (f) ⁻2 and 2

3 (a) (i) 21   (ii) $1\frac{1}{2}$ (iii) ⁻6
   (b) (i) 5   (ii) ⁻$1\frac{1}{2}$ (iii) ⁻4
   (c) (i) $3\frac{1}{2}$ (ii) $\frac{1}{4}$ (iii) ⁻1
   (d) (i) 5   (ii) $11\frac{1}{2}$ (iii) 14

4 (a) {1, 3, 5, 7} (b) {⁻5, ⁻3, ⁻1, 1, 3} (c) {all the odd integers}

2.4 Different types of relations

1 (a) Figure 7(b) (b) Figure 7(c)

2 (a) See Figure K. (b) Many-to-many

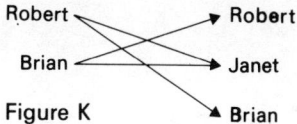

3 See Figure L. Note that different domains could change the type of relations. For example, (d) is many-to-many when the domain is {6, 7, 8, 9, 10}.

(a) $x \longrightarrow$ number of prime factors of x

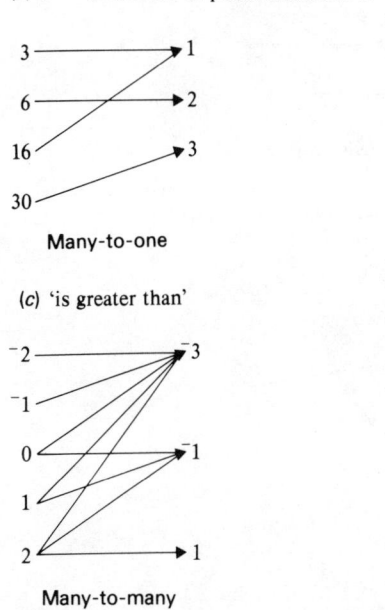

(b) $x \longrightarrow 12/x$

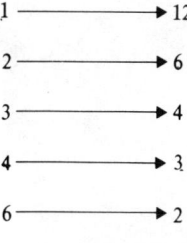

One-to-one

(d) 'is divisible by'

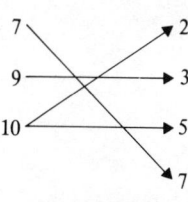

One-to-many

Figure L

Exercise C

1 'is a cousin of' and 'is a granddaughter of' are both many-to-many relations. $x \rightarrow$ number of children of x is a many-to-one relation.

2 (a) See Figure M. (b) Many-to-one

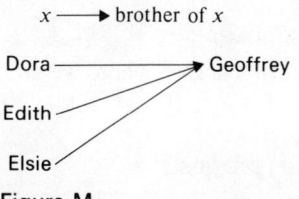

Figure M

31

3 Some examples are 'is the brother of' on {Stephen, Martin}, and 'is the husband of' on {Tom, Jim, Philip, Geoffrey, Jack}. In all one-to-one relations, the number of elements in the domain is equal to the number of elements in the range. This is not true in general for the other types of relations.

4 See Figure N.

(a) $x \to$ largest prime factor of x

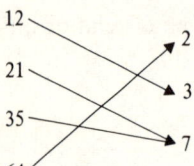

Many-to-one

(b) $x \to x^3$

One-to-one

(c) 'is divisible by'

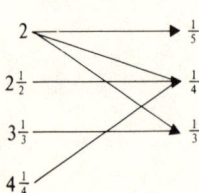

Many-to-many

(d) $x \to$ number of letters in x

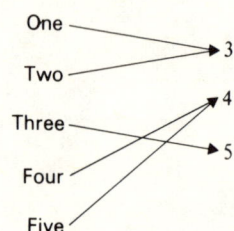

Many-to-one

Figure N

2.5 Inverse relations

1 (a) See Figure O. (b) 'is a grandparent of' or $x \to$ granddaughter of x.

'is a grandparent of'

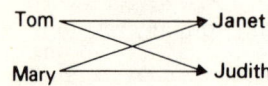

Figure O

2 $x \to 2x$

3 (a) Yes. $x \to x+3$ followed by $x \to x-3$ always takes us back to where we started.
 (b) $x \to x-3$
 (c) $x \to x+3$
 (d) $x \to x$ (This is known as the *identity* (or 'stay put') relation.)

4 (a) $x \to 5x$ (b) $x \to x$

5 (a) See Figure P. (b) 'is the greatest prime factor of'.
(c) Many-to-one

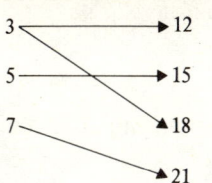

'is the greatest prime factor of'

Figure P

6 (a) and (b) See Figure Q. (c) The two diagrams are the same.

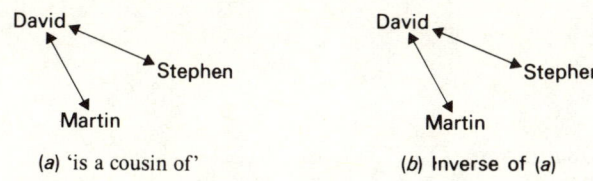

(a) 'is a cousin of' (b) Inverse of (a)

Figure Q

7 (a) See Figure R. (b) This mapping is self-inverse.

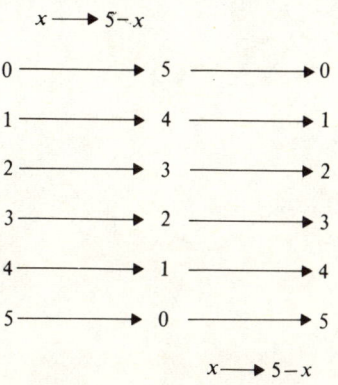

Figure R

Exercise D

1

Relation	Type	Inverse	Type	Self-inverse?
(a)	One-to-one	$x \to x-4$	One-to-one	No
(b)	Many-to-one	$x \to \pm\sqrt{x}$	One-to-many	No
(c)	Many-to-one	$x \to x-\frac{1}{2},\, x$	One-to-many	No
(d)	One-to-one	$x \to 6/x$	One-to-one	Yes
(e)	One-to-one	$x \to x/15$	One-to-one	No

33

2

Relation	Type	Inverse	Type	Self-inverse?
(a)	Many-to-many	x → uncle of x	Many-to-many	No
(b)	One-to-one	x → brother of x	One-to-one	Yes
(c)	Many-to-many	x → {brother or sister of x}	Many-to-many	No
(d)	One-to-many	x → sister of x	Many-to-one	No

The results for (b), (c) and (d) show how the choice of domain can affect the inverse.

Post-test

1   (a) $n \to 3n - 2$
         $0 \to {}^-2$
         $3 \to 7$
         $4 \to 10$
         $6 \to 16$
         $8 \to 22$
  (b) 7   (c) 22   (d) 5   (e) One-to-one   (f) $\{{}^-2, 7, 10, 16, 22\}$
  (g) Domain $\{{}^-2, 7, 10, 16, 22\}$, range $\{0, 3, 4, 6, 8\}$, $n \to \tfrac{1}{3}(n+2)$

2

Relation	Type	Self-inverse?
(a)	Many-to-one	No
(b)	One-to-one	Yes
(c)	One-to-one	No
(d)	One-to-one	Yes
(e)	Many-to-many	No

3   (a) $x \to \tfrac{1}{4}x$, x is 4 times y.
  (b) $x \to 4x$, 'multiply by 4'.
  (c) The relations are not the same. They are an inverse pair.

3 Functions

Objectives

This is what you should be able to do after studying this chapter.
(1) Recognise when a relation is a function.
(2) Use the notation $f: x \to \ldots$ and $f(x) = \ldots$ to represent functions, and the notation f^{-1} to represent inverse functions.
(3) Find the inverse (if any) of a given function.
(4) Show that the functions $x \to k/x$ and $x \to k-x$ are self-inverse.
(5) Use flow diagrams to represent composite functions and their inverses.

Pre-test

1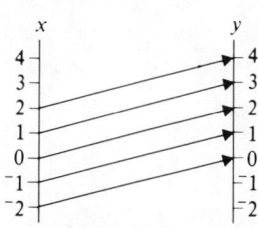

Figure 1

(a) Write the relation shown by the mapping diagram in Figure 1 in three different ways.
(b) What is the set of values of x called?
(c) What is the set of values of y called?
(d) What type of relation is this?

2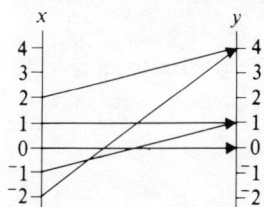

Figure 2

(a) Write the mapping shown in Figure 2 in two different ways.
(b) What type of relation is this?

3 What type of relation is each of the following?
   (a) $x \to$ next largest integer, domain $\{\frac{6}{9}, \frac{8}{9}, \frac{10}{9}, \frac{12}{9}\}$
   (b) $x \to 3^x$, domain $\{1, 2, 3, 4\}$
   (c) $x \to$ nearest integers above and below x (for example, $1\cdot5 \to 1$ and $1\cdot5 \to 2$), domain $\{1\cdot5, 2\cdot5, 3\cdot5, 4\cdot5\}$
   (d) 'is the last digit of the square of', domain $\{0, 1, 4, 5, 6, 9\}$ and range $\{1, 2, 3, 4, 5, 6, 7, 8, 9, 10\}$

3.1 Functions

1 In Chapter 2 we considered four types of relations: one-to-one, one-to-many, many-to-one and many-to-many. Question **3** in the pre-test above contains one example of each.

In which of these does every member of the domain have a unique (only one) image?

You should have listed two types. Figure 3 shows an example of each. Figure 3(a) shows a one-to-one relation, and Figure 3(b) is an example of a many-to-one relation. In both cases, only one arrow leaves each member of the domain (or, put another way, no member of the domain has more than one arrow leaving it), so that if we are asked 'What is the image of *?' there is always a unique answer, whichever member of the domain * stands for.

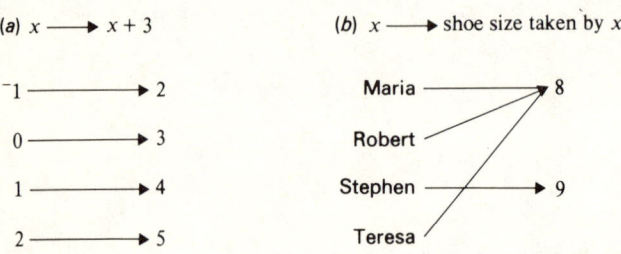

Figure 3

Such relations are given the special name of *functions*. A function, therefore, is either a one-to-one or a many-to-one relation. The important thing is that every member of the domain has a unique image.

2 Draw mapping diagrams for the following relations on the given domains.
   (a) $x \to x^2 + 1$ (b) 'has the same number of sides as'

2	Triangle	Triangle
1	Square	Square
0	Kite	Kite
⁻1	Rectangle	Rectangle

3 (a) What type of relation is $x \to x^2 + 1$? Is it a function?
   (b) What type of relation is 'has the same number of sides as'? Is it a function?

Exercise A

1. Which of the following are functions for the given domains? If they are not functions, give an example to show why they are not.
   (a) $x \to$ largest prime factor of x, domain {12, 21, 35, 64}
   (b) $x \to x^3$, domain {$^-$2, $^-$1, 0, 1, 2}
   (c) $x \to$ number of letters in x, domain {one, two, three, four, five}
   (d) 'is divisible by', domain {2, $2\frac{1}{2}$, $3\frac{1}{3}$, $4\frac{1}{4}$} and range {$\frac{1}{5}$, $\frac{1}{4}$, $\frac{1}{3}$}
   (e) $x \to$ month of x's birthday, for a class of 30 children.
   (f) $x \to$ make of car owned by x, domain {car owners who live in Birmingham}
   (g) $x \to 2x+1$, domain {real numbers between 0 and 1}

2. Identify the relations in the mapping diagrams of Figure 4, state what type of relations they are, and decide whether or not they are functions.

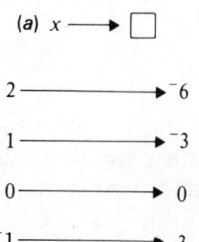
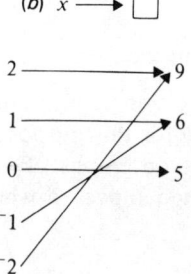
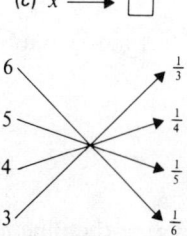
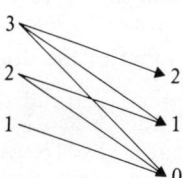

Figure 4

3. (a) Draw the diagram for the relation 'has as a prime factor' over the domain {2, 3, 4, 5}.
   (b) What happens if the number 6 is now added to the domain?

37

3.2 Function notation

Figure 5 shows part of the function 'multiply by 3 and add 1'.

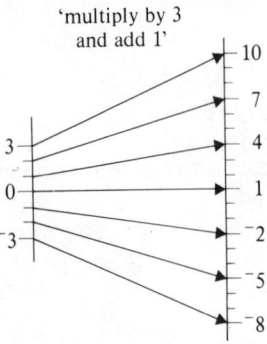

Figure 5

1 Write this function in the form $x \rightarrow \ldots$

It is useful to have a short notation to stand for a function, and we often use letters such as f, g, h for this purpose. (In the same way, we often use letters such as x and y to label axes on graphs.) For example, we may use the letter f to stand for the function illustrated above; in which case we write

$$f: x \rightarrow 3x+1$$

which is read as 'f is the function that maps x onto $3x+1$'. We can also write

$$f(x) = 3x+1$$

which is read as 'the image of x under the function f is $3x+1$', or, more simply, 'f of x equals $3x+1$'.

Thus, given one member of the domain, 11 say, we write

$$f: 11 \rightarrow 34 \quad \text{or} \quad f(11) = 34,$$

and if we were told that $f(x) = 16$, we could work out that $x = 5$.

Some people tend to use the $f: x \rightarrow \ldots$ notation when considering the function in general, and the $f(x) = \ldots$ notation when concentrating on particular members of the domain or range, but this is not essential.

If we wish to consider more than one function at a time, then we use different letters. For example, the function $x \rightarrow 3x+1$ might be shown by the letter f, and the function $x \rightarrow 3(x+1)$ by the letter g.

2 Write g in the form $g: x \rightarrow \ldots$

3 h stands for the function 'multiply by 5, and then subtract 2'.
 (a) Write h in the form $h: x \rightarrow \ldots$
 (b) Work out $h(4)$.
 (c) Work out $h(^-2)$.
 (d) If $h(x) = 18$, what is x?

The inverse is obtained simply by reversing the arrows in the mapping diagram. So if the original function is one-to-one, the inverse is also one-to-one and is still a function (see Figure 10(a) below). However, if the original function is many-to-one, the inverse is a one-to-many relation and is not a function (Figure 10(b)).

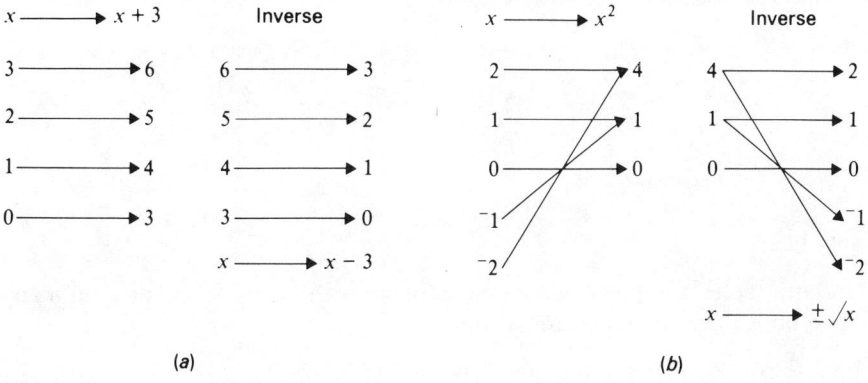

(a)   (b)

Figure 10

Note that in Figure 10(b) we are now including negative numbers in the original domain, and so the inverse is $x \to \pm\sqrt{x}$ (the positive or negative square root of x), which is not a function.

Exercise D

1 Describe in words the inverses of the following functions.
(a) 'add 5'   (b) 'multiply by 8'   (c) 'subtract 9'
(d) 'divide by $1\frac{1}{2}$'   (e) 'cube'

2 Write the inverses of the following in the form $f^{-1}: x \to \ldots$
$a: x \to x + 1\frac{1}{2}$, $b: x \to 10x$, $c: x \to \frac{1}{4}x$, $d: x \to x - 11$, $e: x \to x$

3 Work out $f^{-1}(20)$ for these functions.
(a) $f: x \to 4x$ (b) $f: x \to x - 7$

4 Which of the following functions, considered over the domain of all positive numbers, have an inverse that is a function?
(a) $x \to 3x$ (b) $x \to$ next highest counting number
(c) $x \to 9 - x$ (d) $x \to 2$

3.5 Self-inverse functions

In Chapter 2 we found that some relations are self-inverse, that is, the inverse relation is the same as the orginal relation.

Consider the functions shown in Figure 11 overleaf. In Figure 11(a), we have selected a few examples from a domain of all real numbers, but in Figure 11(b) we have restricted ourselves to a finite domain, although the domain could be all real numbers except zero.

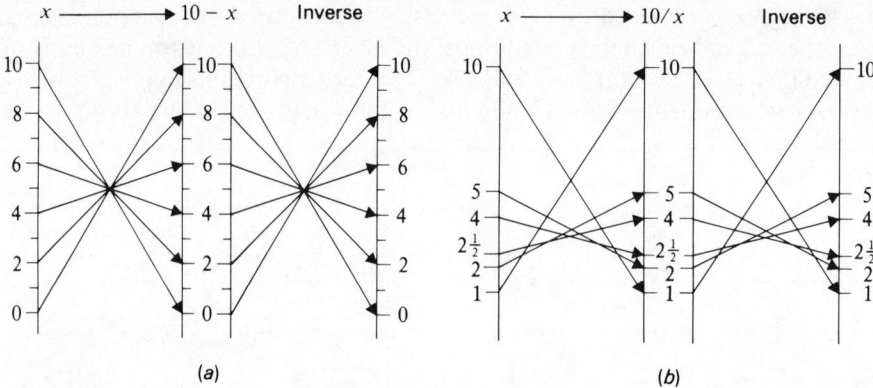

Figure 11

In both these examples, the inverse mapping is the same as the original mapping, and so both these functions are self-inverse.

▷ 1 Check this by completing the flow diagrams of Figure 12.

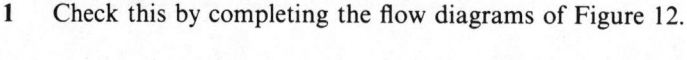

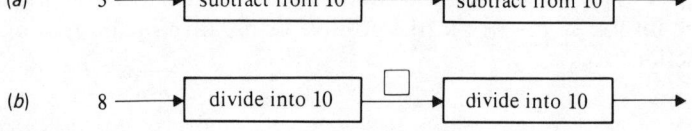

Figure 12

2 If we feed in x in either case, what is the final output?

Exercise E

▷ 1 The function 'subtract from 15' is shown, for the domain of all real numbers, by $s: x \to 15-x$.
  (a) Find the values of $s(3)$ and $s(12)$, $s(6\frac{1}{2})$ and $s(8\frac{1}{2})$, $s(^-7)$ and $s(22)$.
  (b) What can you say about the functions s and s^{-1}?
  (c) State in words the inverse of 'subtract from 15'.
  (d) Are these results true for $x \to k-x$, where k is any real number?

2 Which of the following functions are self-inverse over the domain of all real numbers (except zero)? For those that are not, state the inverse.
  (a) $x \to 12/x$ ('divide into 12')
  (b) $x \to x/12$ ('divide by 12')
  (c) $x \to k/x$, where k is any non-zero number
  (d) $x \to x/k$, where k is any non-zero number

Summary

(1) A function is a relation in which every member of the domain has a unique (only one) image. Thus a function is either a one-to-one or a many-to-one relation.

(2) *Function notation*

    (a) The function 'multiply by 5 and add 2' may be written
$$x \to 5x+2,$$
$f: x \to 5x+2$ (f is the function that maps x onto $5x+2$),
or $f(x) = 5x+2$ (the image of x under f is $5x+2$).

    (b) For an individual member of the domain, such as 11, we can write
$$11 \to 5 \times 11 + 2 = 57, f: 11 \to 57, \text{ or } f(11) = 57.$$

    (c) If more than one function is being considered, other letters are used. It is customary to use the letters f, g, h first.

(3) A composite function is composed of two simpler functions. For example, $x \to 5x+2$ is a combination of 'multiply by 5' and 'add 2'. Its composition can be shown in a flow diagram (see Figure 13).

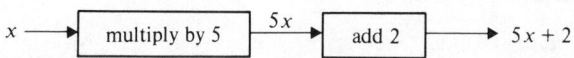

Figure 13

(4) (a) The inverse of a function undoes the effect of the function. If the original function is shown as a mapping diagram, then the inverse is obtained by reversing the direction of the arrows.

    (b) If a function is a one-to-one relation, then the inverse is also a function (and is also one-to-one). If the function is a many-to-one relation, then the inverse is not a function.

    (c) The inverse of a function f is shown by f^{-1}.

(5) (a) In self-inverse functions the inverse is identical to the original function.

    (b) $x \to k-x$ is a self-inverse function over the domain of all real numbers for all values of k.

    (c) $x \to k/x$ is self-inverse for all values of k other than zero over the domain of all non-zero real numbers.

Post-test

1. Which of the following are functions for the domain of positive integers? For those that are not, explain why they are not.
(a) $x \to x^2+2$ (b) $x \to \sqrt{(x+2)}$ (c) $x \to \pm\sqrt{(x+2)}$
(d) $x \to$ largest divisor of x excluding x itself (for example, $33 \to 11$)
(e) $x \to 1/x$ (f) $x \to$ prime factors of x (g) $x \to 100-x$

2. Write the following relations in function notation.
(a) 'multiply by $\frac{1}{2}$ and add 3'   (b) 'cube and subtract from 30'
(c) 'divide into 24'   (d) 'divide by 24'   (e) 'subtract from 1'

3   Draw flow diagrams to illustrate parts (*a*), (*b*) and (*c*) of question **2**.

4   Which of the relations in question **1** have inverses that are functions?

5   Which of the functions in question **2** are self-inverse?

Assignment

1   Which of the following are functions for the domain of positive integers? Express those that are in the form $f: x \to \ldots$
    (*a*) 'add 3 and square'   (*b*) 'multiply by $1\frac{1}{2}$'
    (*c*) 'is the highest prime factor of' when the range is all positive integers
    (*d*) 'has as prime factors' when the range is all positive integers
    (*e*) 'divide into 100'   (*f*) 'cube'

2   Write down in verbal form the inverses of the relations in question **1**. Which of these inverses are functions?

3   Draw flow diagrams to illustrate parts (*a*), (*e*) and (*f*) of question **1**.

4   Which of the relations in question **1** are self-inverse?

5   $f: x \to 4x$, $g: x \to 1-x$ and $h: x \to 16/x$.
    (*a*) Express the inverses of f, g and h in a similar form.
    (*b*) Find the values of $f(5)$, $g(0\cdot 4)$, $h(\frac{1}{2})$, $f^{-1}(5)$, $g^{-1}(0\cdot 4)$, $h^{-1}(\frac{1}{2})$.
    (*c*) Which of these functions are self-inverse?

Answers

Pre-test

1   (*a*) $x \to x+2$, or 'add 2', or x is 2 less than y
    (*b*) Domain   (*c*) Range   (*d*) One-to-one
2   (*a*) $x \to x^2$, or 'square'   (*b*) Many-to-one
3   See Figure A.

(*d*) 'is the last digit in the square of'

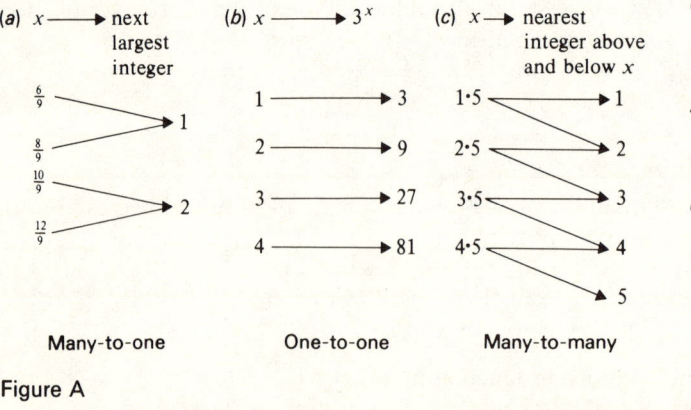

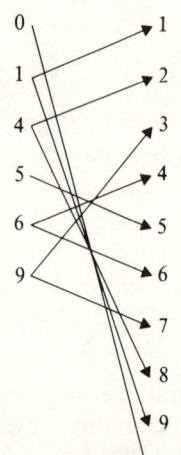

Figure A

One-to-many

3.1 Functions

1. The relations with unique images are one-to-one or many-to-one.
2. See Figure B.
3. (a) $x \to x^2 + 1$ is a many-to-one relation, and so it is a function.
   (b) This is a many-to-many relation, and so it is not a function.

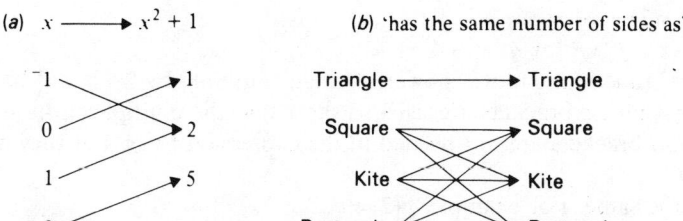

Figure B

Exercise A

1. (a), (b), (c), (e) and (g) are functions. In each case there is only one answer to the question 'What is x mapped onto?'
   (d) is not a function because, for example, 2 is divisible by $\frac{1}{5}$ and $\frac{1}{4}$.
   (f) is not a function because some people may own more than one make of car.

2.

Relation	Type	Is it a function?
(a) $x \to {}^-3x$	One-to-one	Yes
(b) $x \to x^2 + 5$	Many-to-one	Yes
(c) $x \to 1/x$	One-to-one	Yes
(d) x is greater than y	Many-to-many	No

3. (a) See Figure C.
   (b) If 6 is added to the domain, the relation is no longer a function because $6 \to 2$ and $6 \to 3$.

'has as a prime factor'

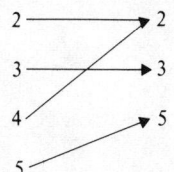

Figure C

3.2 Function notation

1. $x \to 3x + 1$
2. $g: x \to 3(x+1)$
3. (a) $h: x \to 5x - 2$ (b) $h(4) = 18$ (c) $h({}^-2) = {}^-12$
   (d) If $h(x) = 18$, then $5x - 2 = 18$. This means that $5x = 20$, and so $x = 4$.

Exercise B

1. (a) $a: x \to (x/5)+2$ (b) $b: x \to (x+2)/5$ (c) $c: x \to x^2-7$
   (d) $d: x \to (x-7)^2$ (e) $e: x \to 8-x$
   $a(3) = 2\frac{3}{5}$, $b(3) = 1$, $c(3) = 2$, $d(3) = (^-4)^2 = 16$, $e(3) = 5$

2. (a) $p(2)$ is 2 squared ($= 4$), and then doubled ($= 8$). So $p(2) = 8$ and $p(3) = 9 \times 2 = 18$. $q(2)$ is 2 doubled ($= 4$), and then squared ($= 16$). So $q(2) = 16$ and $q(3) = 6^2 = 36$.
   (b) $p: x \to 2x^2$, $q: x \to (2x)^2$ (or $q: x \to 4x^2$)
   As the 'square' function is more 'powerful' than 'multiply by 2', it will be worked out first unless brackets are used to show that the multiplication must be done first. So brackets are not needed in the expression for p, but they are essential for q.
   (c) They are not the same. For example, $p(2) \neq q(2)$.

3.3 Flow diagrams for composite functions

1. (a) See Figure D. (b) $f(2) = 7$, $f(5) = 16$, $g(2) = 9$, $g(5) = 18$
   (c) They are not the same. For example, $f(2) \neq g(2)$.

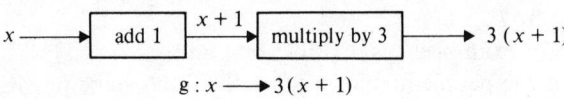

Figure D

Exercise C

1. (a) See Figure E(a). (b) See Figure E(b).
   (c) $a(5) = 3$, $a(8) = 3\frac{3}{5}$, $b(5) = 1\frac{2}{5}$, $b(8) = 2$
   (d) They are not the same.

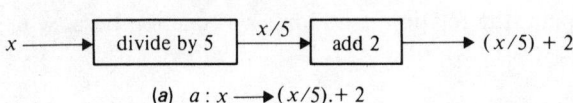

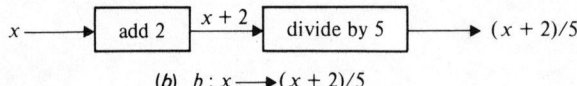

Figure E

2. See Figure F.

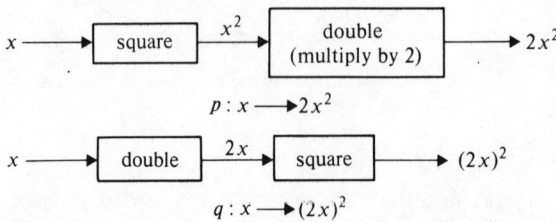

Figure F

3   (a) See Figure G.   (b) $k(0) = 15$, $k(25) = 15 - \sqrt{25} = 10$, $k(400) = 15 - \sqrt{400} = {}^-5$
    (c) $k: x \to 15 - \sqrt{x}$

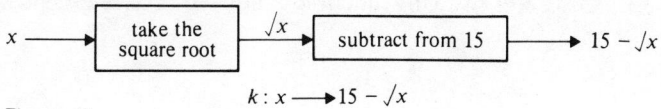

Figure G

3.4 Inverse functions

1   (a) 'divide by 5' (or 'multiply by $\frac{1}{5}$')
    (b) $g^{-1}: x \to x/5$ (or $g^{-1}: x \to \frac{1}{5}x$)
2   (a) $h^{-1}: x \to x+4$ (b) $h^{-1}(3) = 7$

Exercise D

1   (a) 'subtract 5'   (b) 'divide by 8' (or 'multiply by $\frac{1}{8}$')
    (c) 'add 9'   (d) 'multiply by $1\frac{1}{2}$'   (e) '(find the) cube root'
    In (b), both operations are 'reasonable'. Other ways of describing (a) and (d) are 'add $^-5$', and 'divide by $\frac{2}{3}$', but these are less useful ways of expressing these inverses.
2   $a^{-1}: x \to x - 1\frac{1}{2}$, $b^{-1}: x \to x/10$, $c^{-1}: x \to 4x$, $d^{-1}: x \to x+11$, $e^{-1}: x \to x$
    The function e is, in fact, the *identity* function. It is self-inverse (see the next section).
3   (a) $f^{-1}: x \to x/4$, and so $f^{-1}(20) = 5$
    (b) $f^{-1}: x \to x+7$, and so $f^{-1}(20) = 27$
4   The inverses of (a) and (c) are functions. The inverse of (b) is not because, for example, in the original mapping both $1\frac{1}{2}$ and $1\frac{3}{4}$ map onto 2, so that, in the inverse, 2 has many images. The inverse of (d) is not a function because, in the original, all the elements of the domain map onto 2, and so, in the inverse, 2 has an infinite number of images.

3.5 Self-inverse functions

1   See Figure H.
2   In both cases, $x \to x$.

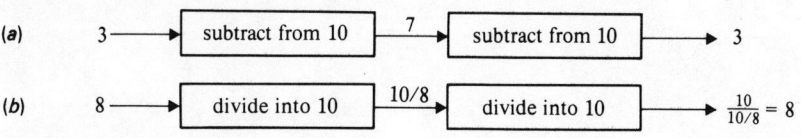

Figure H

Exercise E

1   (a) $s(3) = 12$ and $s(12) = 3$, $s(6\frac{1}{2}) = 8\frac{1}{2}$ and $s(8\frac{1}{2}) = 6\frac{1}{2}$, $s(^-7) = 22$ and $s(22) = ^-7$.
    (b) s and s^{-1} are the same, i.e. s is self-inverse.
    (c) The inverse of 'subtract from 15' is 'subtract from 15'.
    (d) Yes. $x \to k - x$ is self-inverse for all values of k.

2 (*a*) and (*c*) are self-inverse.
   (*b*) The inverse of $x \to x/12$ is $x \to 12x$, so this function is not self-inverse.
   (*d*) The inverse of $x \to x/k$ is $x \to kx$. This function is not self-inverse except when $k = 1$ or $^-1$.

Post-test

  1 (*a*), (*b*) ($\sqrt{(x+2)}$ means the positive square root of $x+2$), (*d*), (*e*), and (*g*) are functions.
   (*c*) $x \to \pm\sqrt{(x+2)}$ is not a function: for example, 7 maps onto 3 and $^-3$. (Note that even if the domain is restricted to positive numbers, the range may contain some negative numbers.)
   (*f*) is not a function: for example, 30 maps onto 2, 3, and 5.
2 (*a*) $x \to \tfrac{1}{2}x+3$ (*b*) $x \to 30-x^3$ (*c*) $x \to 24/x$ (*d*) $x \to x/24$ (*e*) $x \to 1-x$
3 See Figure I.

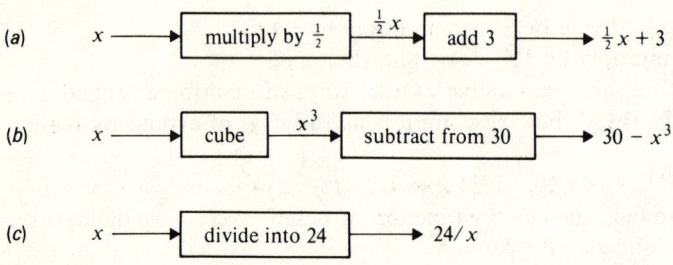

Figure I

4 The inverses of (*b*), (*c*), (*e*) and (*g*) are functions.
5 In question **2**, relations (*c*) and (*e*) are self-inverse.

4 Combining sets and combining functions

Objectives

This is what you should be able to do after studying this chapter.
(1) Define, and illustrate by Venn diagrams, the intersection of two sets and the union of two sets.
(2) Recognise disjoint sets, and the empty set.
(3) Recognise and use the symbols $\cap$, $\cup$, $\emptyset$ and $n(A)$.
(4) Use Venn diagrams to solve simple problems concerned with the number of elements in two or more given sets.
(5) Distinguish between a simple function and a composite function, and represent the composite function 'f followed by g' as gf.
(6) Find the inverse of a composite function (for example, by drawing the appropriate flow diagrams).

Pre-test

1 $S = \{x^2 : 0 < x < 10, x \text{ is an integer}\}$.
   (a) List the elements of the set S.
   (b) Give a verbal description of the set S.

2 For the set S of question **1**, say whether each of the following statements is true or false. If it is false, correct it by changing the set symbol.
   (a) $9 \in S$ (b) $^-4 \in S$ (c) $\{1\} \subset S$
   (d) $8 \in S$ (e) $100 \in S$ (f) $\{1, 4\} \in S$

3 $A = \{\text{letters in the word } London\}$.
   (a) List the elements of A. How many elements are there in A?
   (b) List the subsets of A. Which of these are proper subsets?

4 Draw a Venn diagram to show the relation between
   $$\mathscr{E} = \{^-3, ^-2, ^-1, 0, 1, 2, 3\} \text{ and } N = \{\text{positive whole numbers}\}.$$
   Describe N'.

5 Which of (a), (b) and (c) are functions?
   (a) $x \to 2x + 3$ (b) $x \to x^2$ (c) $x \to 3(4 - 10x)$
   (d) Draw the flow diagrams for parts (a) and (c).
   (e) State the mapping of part (b) in two ways using function notation.

6 State the inverses of the following functions.
   $f: x \to 3x$, $g: x \to x-2$, $h: x \to \frac{1}{2}x$,
   $j: x \to 5+x$, $k: x \to 12-x$, $l: x \to 4/x$.

4.1 Intersection of sets

1 Draw the Venn diagram to illustrate the relation between the sets $V = \{a, e, i, o, u\}$ and $M = \{$letters in the word *mathematics*$\}$ for $\mathscr{E} = \{$letters of the alphabet$\}$.
   Shade the region representing the elements that belong to both of the sets V and M.

   The set of elements common to both V and M is called the *intersection* of V and M. It is denoted by $V \cap M$ (read as 'V intersection M'). Hence, in this example, $V \cap M = \{a, e, i\}$.

2 Notice that $V \cap M$ is a subset of V. Of what other set is it a subset?

3 (a) If $\mathscr{E} = \{$months of the year$\}$, draw the Venn diagram to show the relation between the sets $J = \{$months beginning with the letter $J\}$, and $L = \{$months with 31 days$\}$.
   (b) Shade the region $J \cap L$, and list the elements of this set.
   (c) Now put a dot in the region that contains only June. We are going to express this region in set notation in terms of J and L, by finding two subsets to which June belongs. Copy and complete the following.
         $\{$June$\} \subset \square$.
         $\{$June$\} \not\subset L$, so $\{$June$\} \subset \square$.
         Does any other month belong to both these subsets?
         Hence $\{$June$\} = \square \cap \square$.

4 Now draw the Venn diagram to illustrate L, M and $\mathscr{E}$, where $M = \{$months beginning with the letter $M\}$. Shade $L \cap M$. What is special about $L \cap M$?

Disjoint sets and the empty set

If $F = \{$months beginning with the letter $F\}$, the Venn diagram of Figure 1 shows F and L.

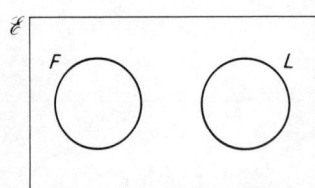

Figure 1

In this case we do not overlap the curves for F and L because there are no months that satisfy both these conditions (begin with the letter F, and have 31 days), i.e. there are no elements in the intersection of F and L. We say that F and L are *disjoint sets*.

Any set that has no members or elements is called the *empty set*. Thus $F \cap L$ is 'the empty set'. We use the Danish letter ø ('oe' – pronounced as the 'ur' in 'fur') to stand for the empty set. Curly brackets are not used, because we think of ø as a capital letter. So $F \cap L = $ ø.

(Some books use the notation { } for the empty set, but this can be confusing. You are advised to use only ø. Note, also, that {ø} does *not* represent the empty set – in fact, it is a set that has one member, the empty set!)

Exercise A

1 Illustrate the relations between the following pairs of sets by drawing Venn diagrams and entering the individual elements.
 (a) $A = $ {vowels}, $B = $ {first five letters of the alphabet}
 (b) $A = \{1, 2, 3, 4\}, B = \{5, 6, 7\}$
 (c) $A = $ {multiples of 2 less than 14}, $B = $ {multiples of 6 less than 25}
 (d) $A = $ {the first four prime numbers}, $B = \{x: x < 10, x$ is a positive integer}

2 For each pair of question **1**, list the members of or define $A \cap B$, $A' \cap B$ and $A \cap B'$.

3 Why is it not necessary to define a universal set for each pair of question **2**?

4 Copy and complete the following.
 (a) $\{\psi, \triangle, *\} \cap \{\bigcirc, \psi, *, +\} = \{\ldots\}$
 (b) $\{a, \square\} \cap \{b, c\} = \{c\}$
 (c) $\{7, 9, \square\} \cap \{5, \square, 2, 3\} = \{9, 3\}$
 (d) $\{d, \square, \square, b, t\} \cap \{p, \square, d, \square\} = \{a, \square, e\}$

5 If A is any set with one or more members, what can you say about these?
 (a) $A \cap \mathscr{E}$ (b) $A \cap A$ (c) $A \cap A'$
 (d) $A \cap $ ø (e) ø $\cap \mathscr{E}$

4.2 Union of sets

Let $\mathscr{E} = $ {new cars for sale at this year's Motor Show}, $A = $ {Austin cars}, and $B = $ {blue cars}. A man wishing to buy a new car at the Show says 'I am looking for a blue car, but I wouldn't mind having an Austin whatever colour it is.'

Figure 2 shows this on a Venn diagram.

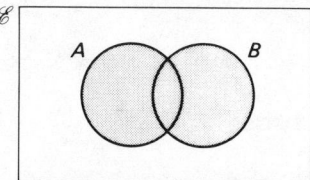

Figure 2

The shaded region represents the cars that are possible buys for the man, because this region covers the members of $\mathscr{E}$ which are Austin cars, or blue cars, or both.

This illustrates another important subset of $\mathscr{E}$ which is called the *union* of the two sets A and B. It is written as $A \cup B$, and read as 'A union B'.

1 Let $\mathscr{E}$ = {letters of the alphabet},
   X = {letters in the word *correspondence*}, and
   Y = {letters in the word *course*}.
   (a) State in words the meaning of $X \cup Y$.
   (b) Draw the appropriate Venn diagram. Shade the union of X and Y. List the members of the union.
   (c) Notice that $X \subset (X \cup Y)$. State two more subsets of $X \cup Y$.

Exercise B

1 Let $\mathscr{E}$ = {letters in the word *cushion*},
   Z = {letters in the word *shun*}, and V = {i, o, u}.
   (a) Draw a Venn diagram to show these sets.
   (b) List the members of V', Z', $V \cup Z$, $V' \cup Z$ and $V \cup Z'$.

2 For each pair of sets in question 1 of exercise A, list the elements of $A \cup B$.

3 Each of the following is equal to a single set, whatever S is. Find that single set.
   (a) $S \cup \mathscr{E}$ (b) $S \cup S$ (c) $S \cup S'$ (d) $S \cup \emptyset$ (e) $\emptyset \cup \mathscr{E}$

4 Make four copies of Figure 3.

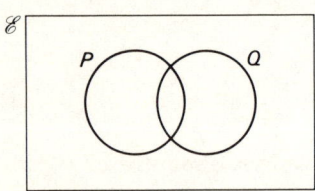

Figure 3

On the first, shade the region representing P'. On the second, shade the region representing Q'. On the third and fourth, show the regions $P' \cap Q'$ and $P' \cup Q'$. What can you say about P and Q in each of the following cases?
(a) $P \cup Q = P$
(b) $(P \cap Q) \subset (P \cup Q)$
(c) $(P' \cup Q') \subset (P' \cap Q')$
(d) $P \cup Q' = P \cap Q$
(e) $P \cap Q = P \cup Q$

4.3 The number of elements in sets and subsets

1 (a) Draw the Venn diagram to show the sets A = {△, ×, θ, *} and B = {□, +, ×}.
   (b) Set A has four members, and this is shown by writing $n(A) = 4$. Calculate the following.
   $$n(B), n(A \cap B), n(A \cup B)$$
   (c) Does $n(A \cap B) = n(A \cup B)$?

2 (*a*) Calculate the following for the sets *X* and *Y* of question **1** of Section 4.2.

$n(X), n(Y), n(X \cap Y), n(X \cup Y)$

(*b*) What connection, if any, do you notice between your answers?

We can use Venn diagrams to solve problems. Here are two examples to show how this can be done.

Example 1. In a class of 33 children, 18 learn Russian, 23 learn German and 11 learn both languages. How many children do not learn either language?

You will probably answer this question like this.
Altogether, 18 children learn Russian, and 23 learn German.
Of these, 11 learn German as well, 11 learn Russian also.
So 7 learn Russian only, and 12 learn German only.
Hence the total number of different children learning a language is

11 (who learn both) + 7 (who learn Russian only)
+ 12 (who learn German only) = 30.

And so the number who learn neither language is $33 - 30 = 3$.

We can show these results on a Venn diagram (see Figure 4). Let $\mathscr{E}$ = {children in the class}, R = {children who learn Russian}, and G = {children who learn German}. (Note that both R and G contain the 11 children who learn both languages.)

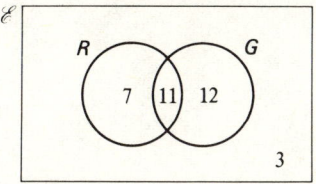

Figure 4

This time we do not show the individual children on the Venn diagram, but instead in each region or subset we put the *number* of elements (children) in that subset. (This might occasionally be confusing, but it is usually obvious whether the numbers on a Venn diagram are the actual elements, or the number of elements in that region.) Numbers entered in this way show the number of elements in *one* region only. The set R and the set G each cover *two* of the regions of the Venn diagram in Figure 4. If we want to show that $n(R) = 18$ and $n(G) = 23$, the usual method is to write the numbers as shown in Figure 5.

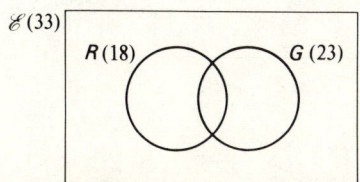

Figure 5

Example 2. In an interview, 50 people were asked which television channels they had watched the previous evening. The results were:
32 watched BBC 1, 33 watched ITV, and 13 watched BBC 2.
9 people watched BBC 1 and BBC 2. Of these, 5 watched ITV as well.
3 watched only BBC 2, and 12 watched ITV only.

Let $\mathscr{E}$ = {the people interviewed}, X = {people who watched BBC 1}, Y = {people who watched BBC 2}, and Z = {people who watched ITV}.

The Venn diagram is shown in Figure 6. To shorten the work a little we have labelled the separate regions with the letters a to h. (Although each region *is* a set, we have used small letters for them to distinguish them from the other sets.)

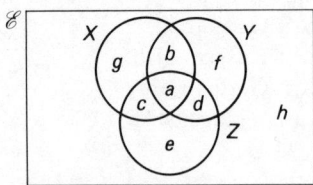

Figure 6

From the information above, we know that $n(a) = 5$, and hence $n(b) = 4$ (the 9 who watched both BBC 1 and BBC 2, minus the 5 who watched all three channels), $n(f) = 3$, and $n(e) = 12$. So we can now fill these in (see Figure 7).

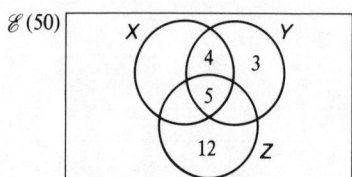

Figure 7

▷ 3 Try to complete Figure 7.

4 (a) How many people watched only BBC 1?
   (b) How many watched BBC 1 and ITV, but not BBC 2?
   (c) How many said that they did not watch television?

Exercise C

▷ 1 Copy and complete the table below for the four pairs of sets A and B in question **1** of Exercise A.

	$n(A)$	$n(B)$	$n(A \cap B)$	$n(A \cup B)$	$n(A)+n(B)$
(a)					
(b)					
(c)					
(d)					

2 Answer these questions from the table for question 1.
   (a) Is it always true that $n(A)+n(B) = n(A \cap B)$?
   (b) Is it always true that $n(A)+n(B) = n(A \cup B)$?
   (c) State a result that is always true.
   (d) When is it true that $n(A \cap B) < n(A)$?
   (e) Complete the following statement so that it is always true.

   $$n(A \cap B) \,\square\, n(A)$$

3 If $n(M) = 6$, and $n(N) = 19$, state the value of $n(M \cup N)$ when (a) $n(M \cap N) = 4$, (b) $n(M \cap N) = 0$.

4 In a group of 30 people, 19 play tennis, 13 play basketball, and 6 play neither. Draw a Venn diagram to show the sets $B = \{$basketball players$\}$ and $T = \{$tennis players$\}$. Find the value of $n(B \cap T)$.

5 A paper-boy delivers 27 copies of the *Daily Mirror* and 22 copies of the *Guardian* in a street of 40 houses.
   Assuming that no house receives more than one copy of each paper, what is (a) the smallest and (b) the largest number of houses that could have two papers delivered?

4.4 Composite functions

In Chapter 3 we looked at the result of combining two mappings.

1 (a) Draw a flow diagram to show what happens to 5 when it is fed through a 'multiply by 3' machine, and the result is then fed through a 'subtract 2' machine.
   (b) Copy and complete the following.
      5 is the ..., 13 is the ..., 5 is ... onto 13.
   (c) Is the mapping a function? Why?

If there is only one operation involved, and therefore only one box in the flow diagram (as, for example, in 'add 4'), then the function is called a *simple function*. But where more than one operation is involved – as in the flow diagram and function above – the function is called a *composite function*.

Suppose we put f for the 'multiply by 3' function, and g for the 'subtract 2' function (so $f: x \to 3x$ and $g: x \to x-2$). If we apply the function f to 5, we get $f(5) = 15$. Applying the function g to this, we get $g(15) = 13$. But 15 is $f(5)$, and so we can replace the 15 in $g(15)$ by $f(5)$ to give $g[f(5)] = 13$. We write $g[f(x)]$ as $gf(x)$, and so in the example above the composite function 'multiply by 3 and subtract 2' is denoted by gf.

2 Express gf in function notation in two ways.

3 (a) Draw the flow diagram for fg (which means 'the function g followed by the function f').
   (b) Find the value of $fg(5)$.
   (c) Is fg the same function as gf?
   (d) Write fg in the form $fg: x \to \ldots$

4   Answer the following for the composite function $h: x \to (x/3)^2$.
   (a) Write down in words the first operation that we must apply.
   (b) What is the second operation?
   (c) Draw the flow diagram for h.
   (d) Find the values of $h(9)$ and $h(^-33)$.
   (e) If $h = fg$, write f and g in the form $f: x \to \ldots$

5   The composite function k is made from the same operations as h, but they are applied in the opposite order.
   (a) Draw the flow diagram for k.
   (b) Find the values of $k(9)$ and $k(^-33)$.
   (c) Write k in the form $k: x \to \ldots$
   We see, then, that the same two operations can lead to different results if we change the order in which they are applied. Therefore, when we write down the expression for a composite function, we must make sure that the order of operations is quite clear. We can always do this by using brackets. For example, $3(x-2)$ means 'first subtract 2, and then multiply by 3', and $(3x)-2$ means 'first multiply by 3, and then subtract 2'.
   However, there are certain conventions (or rules made up for convenience) that are used to avoid using too many brackets.

6   (a) Is $1+3x$ the same as $1+(3x)$ or $(1+3)x$?
   (b) Is $2x^3$ the same as $2(x^3)$ or $(2x)^3$?
   (c) Is $5/x-1$ the same as $(5/x)-1$ or $5/(x-1)$?

Exercise D

1   Evaluate the following for $x = 8$.
   (a) $3-x$ (b) $\tfrac{1}{4}x+5$ (c) $\dfrac{5x+2}{6}$ (d) $\dfrac{30}{21-2x}$ (e) $(-2x+10)^2$

2   Write the following in function notation.
   (a) 'divide by 4 and add 3'
   (b) 'square and subtract 5'
   (c) 'add 7 and multiply by 2'
   (d) 'divide by 2 and square'
   (e) 'add 3, square, and divide by 6'

3   If $p: x \to x-4$ and $q: x \to 2x$, find these.
   (a) $pq(7)$ (b) $pq(1)$ (c) $qp(7)$ (d) $qp(1)$
   Copy and complete: $pq: x \to \ldots$ and $qp: x \to \ldots$

4   For $f: x \to 3x$ and $g: x \to \tfrac{1}{2}x$, find the following.
   (a) $fg(5)$ (b) $fg(^-4)$ (c) $gf(5)$ (d) $gf(^-4)$
   What do you notice? Explain your results by expressing fg and gf in the forms $fg: x \to \ldots$ and $gf: x \to \ldots$

5   If $h = fg$, find f and g in each of the following.
   (a) $h: x \to 2x+3$ (b) $h: x \to (x-7)^2$
   (c) $h: x \to 5+1/x$ (d) $h: x \to 10-x/3$
   (e) $h: x \to \sin(x+30)°$

6 Draw the flow diagrams for f, g, fg and gf when $f: x \to x^2$ and $g: x \to 3x+1$. Hence or otherwise find these.
   (a) $fg(3)$ and $gf(3)$ (b) $fg(^-2)$ and $gf(^-2)$ (c) $fg(x)$ and $gf(x)$

7 Draw a flow diagram to show how $f: x \to (4x-1)^2+7$ can be formed from four simple functions.
   If $f = pqrs$, find the functions p, q, r and s.

4.5 Inverses of composite functions

1 (a) Copy Figure 8. Complete the left-hand side of the arrow diagram to show the function
       $f: x \to 2x+3$ for the domain $\{^-3, ^-2, \ldots, 2, 3\}$.

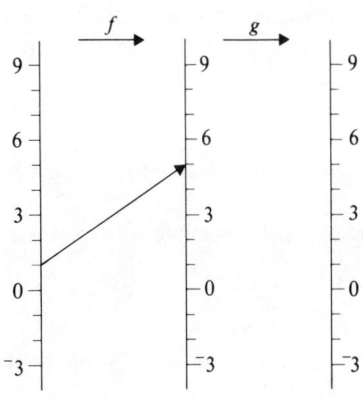

Figure 8

   (b) What is the range of f? This now becomes the domain for the function g.
   (c) If $g: x \to \frac{1}{2}(x-3)$, complete the right-hand side of the diagram.
   (d) What do you notice about the domain of f and the range of g? What is the connection between f and g?

The flow diagram for f is shown in Figure 9(a), and Figure 9(b) shows the 'reversed' flow diagram (working backwards and undoing everything). Rewriting this reversed diagram to read from left to right, we obtain Figure 9(c).

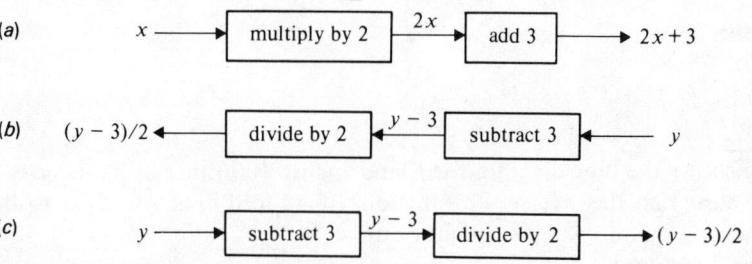

Figure 9

2 Draw the flow diagram for g and compare it with the flow diagram in Figure 9(c).

3 You should have found that the last two flow diagrams were the same. Does it matter that we have used x in one and y in the other? Is it true that 'divide by 2' is the same as 'multiply by ½'? Does $\dfrac{y-3}{2} = \tfrac{1}{2}(y-3)$?

Since g undoes the effect of f (as seen in the arrow diagram), then g is the inverse of f ($g = f^{-1}$). So the reversed flow diagram for f is, in fact, the flow diagram for the inverse of f.

Thus in drawing the flow diagram for the inverse of a composite function we must remember to do two things:
(1) give the inverse of each operation, and
(2) reverse the *order* of the operations.

(This is quite sensible, in fact. When we consider the operations of putting on a sock and then putting on a shoe, the inverse is to take *off* the *shoe* first, and then take off the sock.)

We now have a method for finding the inverse of a composite function f.
(1) Draw the flow diagram for f.
(2) Reverse this, putting in the inverse operations, to obtain the flow diagram for the inverse.
(3) From this reversed flow diagram, write down, where possible, the expression for f^{-1}.

Here are a few examples.

Example 1. Draw the flow diagrams for $f: x \to \dfrac{6x-5}{11}$ and its inverse. Is the inverse a function?

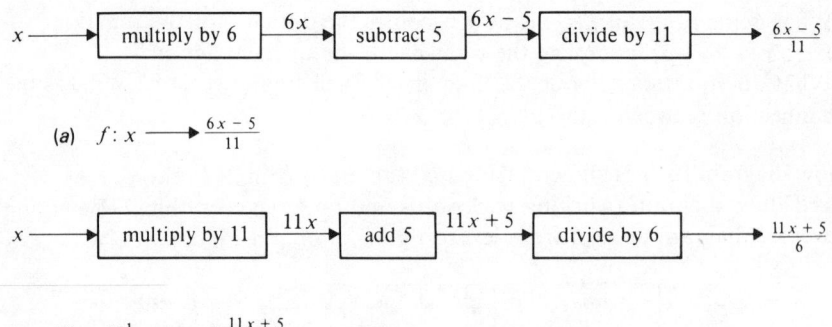

Figure 10

Figure 10(a) shows the flow diagram for f, and Figure 10(b) that of its inverse. It should be clear that the inverse *is* a function. (If we feed in any number to the reversed flow diagram, do we get a unique answer?)

The inverse function is
$$f^{-1}: x \to \dfrac{11x+5}{6}.$$

Example 2. What is the inverse of $g: x \to (3+\tfrac{1}{2}x)^2$? Is it a function?

```
x ─► [multiply by ½] ─½x─► [add 3] ─3+½x─► [square] ─► (3+½x)²
```

(a) $g: x \longrightarrow (3 + \tfrac{1}{2}x)^2$

```
x ─► [take the square root] ─±√x─► [subtract 3] ─±√x−3─► [multiply by 2] ─► 2(±√x − 3)
```

(b) $g^{-1}: x \longrightarrow 2(\pm\sqrt{x} - 3)$

Figure 11

Figure 11(a) shows the flow diagram for g, and Figure 11(b) that of its inverse.
 Remember that the square root of x has two values (for example, the square root of 4 is either 2 or $^-2$, since 2^2 and $(^-2)^2$ are both equal to 4). Thus the inverse is not a function. For example, if $g(x) = 4$, then the reversed flow diagram gives two possible values for x, $2(\pm\sqrt{4}-3) = ^-2$ or $^-10$.
 The inverse mapping is $x \to 2(\pm\sqrt{x}-3)$.

Example 3. If $h: x \to \dfrac{12}{x} - 5$, find $h^{-1}(x)$ and hence $h^{-1}(^-2)$.

 The flow diagram for h is shown in Figure 12(a). Remembering that 'divide into' is a self-inverse function, so that the inverse of $x \to 12/x$ is $x \to 12/x$, we obtain the flow diagram for the inverse as shown in Figure 12(b). Therefore $h^{-1}: x \to \dfrac{12}{x+5}$, and $h^{-1}(^-2) = \dfrac{12}{3} = 4$.

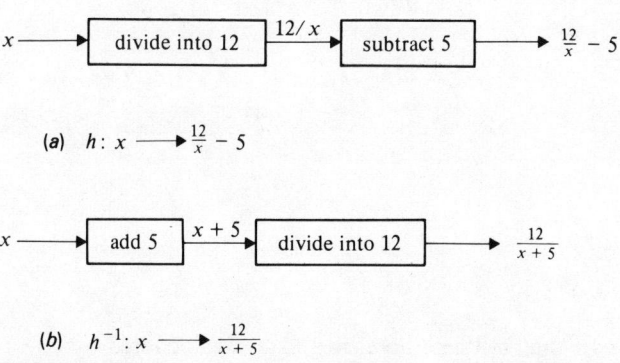

```
x ─► [divide into 12] ─12/x─► [subtract 5] ─► 12/x − 5
```

(a) $h: x \longrightarrow \tfrac{12}{x} - 5$

```
x ─► [add 5] ─x+5─► [divide into 12] ─► 12/(x+5)
```

(b) $h^{-1}: x \longrightarrow \dfrac{12}{x+5}$

Figure 12

Exercise E

1. Find the inverses of the following functions.
   (a) $x \to 3x+5$ (b) $x \to x/5-2$ (c) $x \to 4(x+7)$
   (d) $x \to \dfrac{2x+3}{5}$ (e) $x \to 2x^2+1$ (f) $x \to 6(3-x)$
   (g) $x \to x^3/10-7$ (h) $x \to 3+\sqrt{x}$ (i) $x \to 1-\dfrac{1}{1-x}$

   Which of these inverses are functions?

2. (a) If $f: x \to x-3$ and $g: x \to 7x$, write down the inverses of f and g in the form $f^{-1}: x \to \ldots$
   (b) Find $f(5), g(5), fg(5), gf(5), f^{-1}(5), g^{-1}(5), (fg)^{-1}(5), (gf)^{-1}(5), f^{-1}g^{-1}(5), g^{-1}f^{-1}(5)$.
   (c) What special results do you notice?

Summary

(1) The intersection of two sets A and B is the set of elements that belong to both A and B, and is written $A \cap B$. (See Figure 13(a).)

(2) The union of two sets A and B is the set of elements that belong to A or to B (or to both), and is written $A \cup B$. (See Figure 13(b).)

(3) Two sets which do not intersect (have no elements in common) are said to be disjoint sets. (See Figure 13(c).)

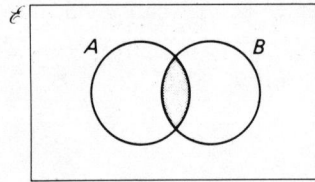

(a) $A \cap B$

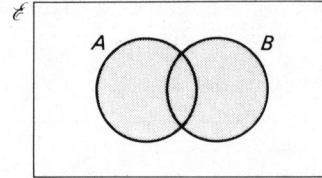

(b) $A \cup B$

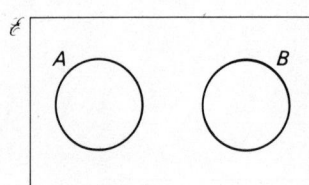

(c) A, B disjoint

Figure 13

(4) The empty set is the set that contains no elements, and is denoted by ø.

(5) In a Venn diagram showing more than one region, we may *either* enter the individual elements in the appropriate regions, *or* write down in each region the number of elements in that region.

(6) $n(A)$ means the number of elements in the set. A. For two sets A and B,

$$n(A)+n(B)-n(A \cap B) = n(A \cup B).$$

(7) A simple function involves one operation only. For an example, see Figure 14(a).

A composite function is composed from more than one function. For an example, see Figure 14(b).

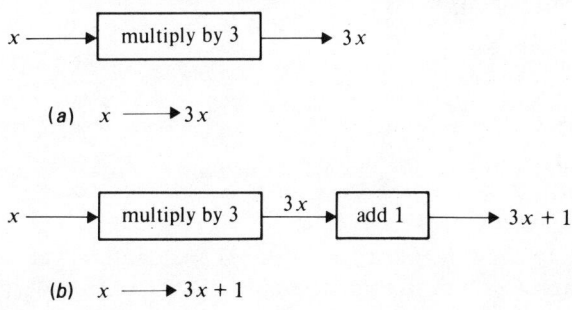

Figure 14

(8) If a composite function h is formed from two simple functions f and g by applying f first followed by g, then $h = gf$.

$gf(x)$ is the image of x after first applying f and then applying g.

$$x \xrightarrow{f} f(x) \xrightarrow{g} gf(x)$$

(9) An inverse flow diagram uses the inverse of each operation in the reverse order. For example, for $f: x \to 3x+1$, the inverse flow diagram is as shown in Figure 15. The inverse function in this example is $f^{-1}: x \to (x-1)/3$ or $f^{-1}(x) = \tfrac{1}{3}(x-1)$.

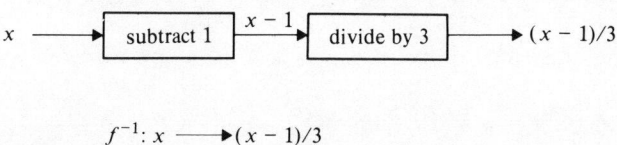

Figure 15

Post-test

1. (a) $P = \{1, 2, 3, 4, 5\}$, $Q = \{2, 4, 6, 8\}$ and $R = \{6, 8, 10\}$. Illustrate these sets in a Venn diagram with $\mathscr{E} = \{$counting numbers $\leqslant 10\}$.
   (b) List the elements of, or define, the sets $P \cap Q$, $P \cap R$, $Q \cap R$, $P \cup Q$ and $Q \cup R$.
   (c) Name a pair of disjoint sets.
   (d) Write down the values of $n(P)$, $n(P \cap R)$ and $n(Q \cup R)$.
   (e) If $n(S) = 7$ and $n(Q \cup S) = 9$, what is $n(Q \cap S)$?

2. (a) If $f: x \to (4x-3)/7$, and $f = ghj$, express the simple functions g, h and j in the form $f: x \to \ldots$
   (b) Draw the inverse flow diagram for f, and find $f^{-1}(3)$ and $f^{-1}(x)$.

3 (a) Draw the flow diagrams for f and f^{-1} if $f: x \to \frac{1}{2}(9x-4)$.
   (b) Obtain f^{-1} in the form $f^{-1}: x \to \ldots$ and find the values of $f(2)$, $f^{-1}(7)$, $f(-\frac{1}{2})$, $f^{-1}(-4\frac{1}{4})$.
   Show how you can use these results to solve equations (c) and (d).
   (c) $f(x) = 7$ (this is $\frac{1}{2}(9x-4) = 7$)   (d) $f(x) = {}^-4\frac{1}{4}$
   (e) Now solve the equation $\frac{1}{2}(9x-4) = {}^-6\frac{1}{2}$.

Assignment

1 Two sets A and B are disjoint, and contain 3 and 5 elements respectively. State the values of $n(A \cap B)$ and $n(A \cup B)$.

2 (a) Draw a Venn diagram to show $E = \{$even numbers$\}$, $O = \{$odd numbers$\}$, $P = \{$prime numbers$\}$ for $\mathscr{E} = \{$positive whole numbers less than 10$\}$.
   (b) Make two copies of this Venn diagram and shade the areas representing $\{3, 5, 7\}$ and $\{2, 3, 4, 5, 6, 7, 8\}$. Express these sets in terms of P and E only.
   (c) Evaluate $n(P)$, $n(P \cap O)$, $n(P \cup E)$.
   (d) What is $O \cap E$?

3 State whether the following statements are always true, sometimes true, never true or nonsense.
   (a) $x \in A \Rightarrow x \in (A \cap B)$ (b) $x \in A \Rightarrow x \in (A \cup B)$
   (c) $P \cup Q = Q \cup P$ (d) $P \cap P = P^2$
   (e) $P \cup Q = Q \cap P$ (f) $P \subset (P \cap Q)'$
   ($x \Rightarrow y$ means if x is true, then y is true as well.)

4 Draw the flow diagrams for the following functions and their inverses.
   (a) $f: x \to 2(6-5x)$ (b) $g: x \to (2x^3-4)/3$
   State the inverse relation in each case. Are the inverses functions?

5 (a) Find the simple functions p, q and r such that $f = pqr$ for $f: x \to \dfrac{13}{2+x} - 5$.
   (b) Draw the flow diagram for f^{-1}, and use it to find $f^{-1}(-18)$ and $f^{-1}(x)$.

6 Use the results you obtained in questions 4 and 5 to solve these equations.
   (a) $\dfrac{13}{2+x} - 5 = {}^-18$
   (b) $2(6-5x) = {}^-8$
   (c) $(2x^3-4)/3 = 4$

Answers

Pre-test

1 (a) $S = \{1, 4, 9, 16, 25, 36, 49, 64, 81\}$
   (b) $S = \{$square numbers less than 100$\}$ or
       $S = \{$the squares of the first nine positive integers$\}$ etc.

2 (a) and (c) are true.
(b) $^-4 \notin S$ (d) $8 \notin S$ (e) $100 \notin S$ (f) $\{1, 4\} \subset S$

3 (a) $A = \{d, l, n, o\}$ (the order of the letters does not matter). There are 4 elements or members in A.
(b) $\{d\}, \{l\}, \{n\}, \{o\}, \{d, l\}, \{d, n\}, \{d, o\}, \{l, n\}, \{l, o\}, \{n, o\}, \{d, l, n\}, \{d, l, o\}, \{d, n, o\}$ and $\{l, n, o\}$ are all proper subsets of A.

The set $\{d, l, n, o\}$ and the set containing no elements are also subsets of A, but they are not proper subsets.

4 See Figure A.

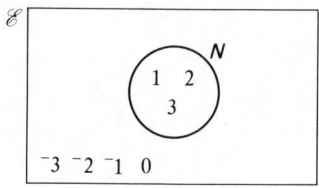

Figure A

$N' = \{^-3, ^-2, ^-1, 0\}$
$= \{\text{non-positive integers}\}$
$= \{\text{negative integers and zero}\}$

5 (a), (b) and (c) are all functions.
(d) See Figure B.
(e) $f: x \to x^2, f(x) = x^2$

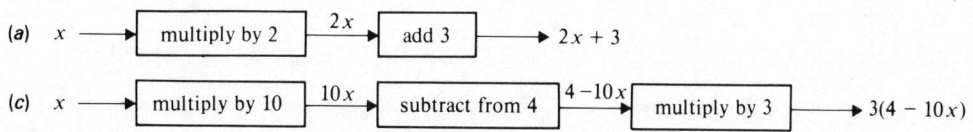

Figure B

6 $f^{-1}: x \to x/3$, $g^{-1}: x \to x+2$, $h^{-1}: x \to 2x$, $j^{-1}: x \to x-5$ (or $x \to ^-5+x$),
$k^{-1}: x \to 12-x$, $l^{-1}: x \to 4/x$
Note that k and l are self-inverse.

4.1 Intersection of sets

1 See Figure C.

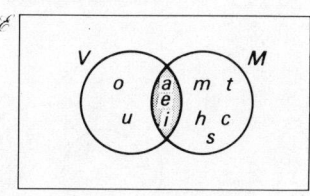

$\mathscr{E} = \{\text{letters of the alphabet}\}$
$V \cap M$ is shaded

Figure C

2   $V \cap M$ is also a subset of M.

3   (a) See Figure D.
    (b) $J \cap L = \{\text{January, July}\}$
    (c) $\{\text{June}\} \subset J$ and $\{\text{June}\} \subset L'$. No other month belongs to both of these subsets, so $\{\text{June}\} = J \cap L'$.

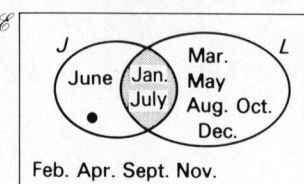

$J \cap L$ is shaded

Figure D

4   See Figure E. $L \cap M = M$ because $M \subset L$.

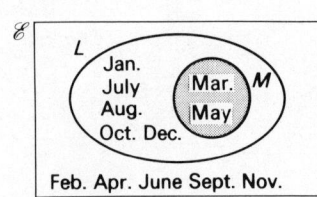

$L \cap M$ is shaded

Figure E

Exercise A

1   See Figure F.

(a) 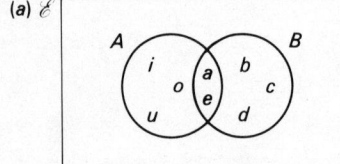   (b) 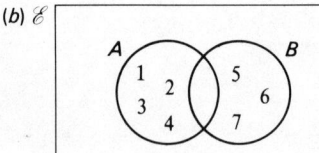   or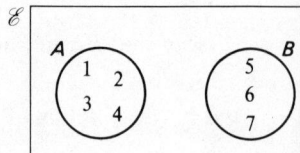

(c) 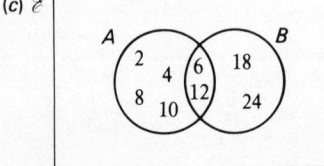   (d) 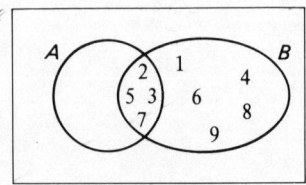   or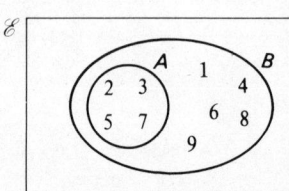

Figure F

2

	$A \cap B$	$A' \cap B$	$A \cap B'$
(a)	{a, e}	{b, c, d}	{i, o, u}
(b)	ø	B	A
(c)	{6, 12}	{18, 24}	{2, 4, 8, 10}
(d)	A	{1, 4, 6, 8, 9}	ø

Note that in part (b) A and B are disjoint sets.

3 Although we cannot define A' and B' without knowing $\mathscr{E}$, we can define $A' \cap B$ and $A \cap B'$ as neither of these subsets contains elements that are not in either A or B.

4 (a) {ψ, *} (Elements of sets do not have to be letters, numbers or words!)
  (b) {a, c} ∩ {b, c} = {c}
  (c) {7, 9, 3} ∩ {5, 9, 2, 3} = {9, 3}
  (d) {d, a, e, b, t} ∩ {p, a, d, e} = {a, d, e}

5 (a) $A \cap \mathscr{E} = A$ (b) $A \cap A = A$ (c) $A \cap A' = ø$
  (d) $A \cap ø = ø$ (e) $ø \cap \mathscr{E} = ø$

4.2 Union of sets

1 (a) $X \cup Y$ is the set of letters that are used in the words *correspondence course*.
  (b) See Figure G.
     $X \cup Y = \{c, d, e, n, o, p, r, s, u\}$ (The letters may be in any order.)
  (c) $Y \subset (X \cup Y)$ and $(X \cap Y) \subset (X \cup Y)$

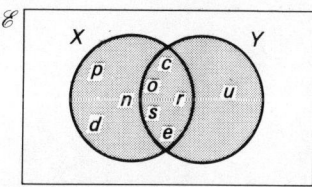

$\mathscr{E}$ = { letters of the alphabet }
$X \cup Y$ is shaded

Figure G

Exercise B

1 (a) See Figure H.
  (b) $V' = \{c, h, n, s\}$, $Z' = \{c, i, o\}$, $V \cup Z = \{h, i, n, o, s, u\}$, $V' \cup Z = \{c, h, n, s, u\}$,
     $V \cup Z' = \{c, i, o, u\}$

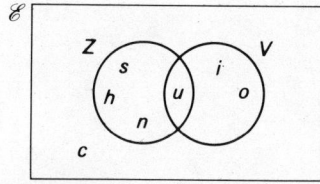

Figure H

2 (a) {a, b, c, d, e, i, o, u} (b) {1, 2, 3, 4, 5, 6, 7}
  (c) {2, 4, 6, 8, 10, 12, 18, 24} (d) {1, 2, 3, 4, 5, 6, 7, 8, 9}

3 (a) $S \cup \mathscr{E} = \mathscr{E}$ (b) $S \cup S = S$ (c) $S \cup S' = \mathscr{E}$
  (d) $S \cup \emptyset = S$ (e) $\emptyset \cup \mathscr{E} = \mathscr{E}$

4 Figure I(a) shows the region P' and Figure I(b) shows Q'. If we overlap these we get Figure I(c), from which we can see that the intersection $P' \cap Q'$ (the elements that belong to both P' and Q') is as in Figure I(d). Note that this is $(P \cup Q)'$. We also see from Figure I(c) that the union $P' \cup Q'$ (the elements that belong to P' or Q' or both) is as in Figure I(e). Note that this is $(P \cap Q)'$.
  (a) If $P \cup Q = P$, then Q is a subset of P, i.e. $Q \subset P$.
  (b) This is always true! Note that if $(P \cup Q) \subset (P \cap Q)$ then $P = Q$.
  (c) $P' \cap Q'$ is always a subset of $P' \cup Q'$. Hence if $(P' \cup Q') \subset (P' \cap Q')$, then there are no elements in the shaded regions of Figure I(f), and so $P = Q$.
  (d) If $P \cup Q' = P \cap Q$, then $Q = \mathscr{E}$.
  (e) If $P \cap Q = P \cup Q$, then, again, $P = Q$.

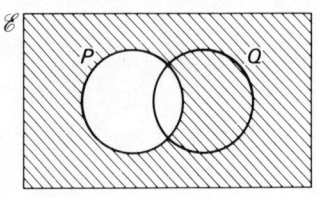
(a) P' is shaded

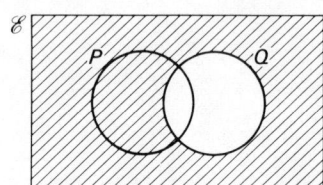
(b) Q' is shaded

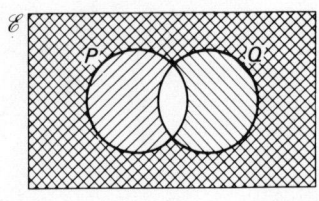
(c)

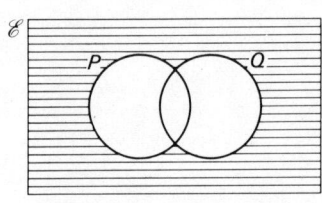
(d) $P' \cap Q' = (P \cup Q)'$ is shaded

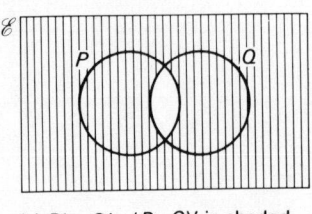
(e) $P' \cup Q' = (P \cap Q)'$ is shaded

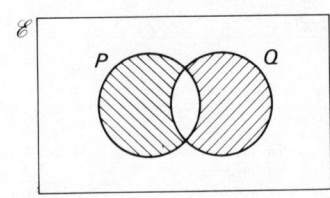
(f)

Figure I

4.3 The number of elements in sets and subsets

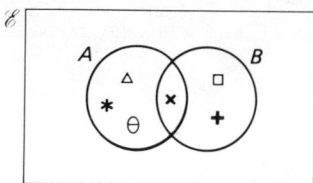

Figure J

1. (a) See Figure J.
   (b) $n(B) = 3$, $n(A \cap B) = 1$, $n(A \cup B) = 6$
   (c) $n(A \cap B) \neq n(A \cup B)$
2. (a) $n(X) = 8$, $n(Y) = 6$, $n(X \cap Y) = 5$, $n(X \cup Y) = 9$
   (b) $n(X) + n(Y) = n(X \cap Y) + n(X \cup Y)$, or $n(X \cup Y) = n(X) + n(Y) - n(X \cap Y)$
3. As $n(Y) = 13$, then $n(d) = 13 - (3 + 4 + 5) = 1$.
   As $n(Z) = 33$, then $n(c) = 33 - (5 + 1 + 12) = 15$. Similarly $n(g) = 8$.

The diagram now becomes as in Figure K. This accounts for $(8 + 15 + 4 + 5) + 3 + 1 + 12 = 48$ people, and so there were 2 people who watched none of the channels ($n(h) = 2$).

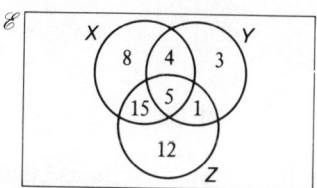

Figure K

4. (a) 8 people (region g) (b) 15 people (region c) (c) 2 people (region h)

Exercise C

1.

	$n(A)$	$n(B)$	$n(A \cap B)$	$n(A \cup B)$	$n(A) + n(B)$
(a)	5	5	2	8	10
(b)	4	3	0	7	7
(c)	6	4	2	8	10
(d)	4	9	4	9	13

2. (a) No (b) No (c) $n(A) + n(B) = n(A \cap B) + n(A \cup B)$
   (d) If $n(A \cap B) < n(A)$, then some of the elements in A do not belong to B.
   (e) $n(A \cap B)$ can never be more than $n(A)$, hence $n(A \cap B) \leq n(A)$.
3. $n(M \cup N) = n(M) + n(N) - n(M \cap N)$
   (a) $n(M \cup N) = 25 - 4 = 21$ (b) $n(M \cup N) = 25 - 0 = 25$

4   See Figure L. As 6 people play neither game, $n(B \cup T) = 30 - 6 = 24$.
Hence $n(B \cap T) = n(B) + n(T) - n(B \cup T) = 13 + 19 - 24 = 8$.
Therefore the number who play tennis only is $19 - 8 = 11$, and who play basketball only is $13 - 8 = 5$.

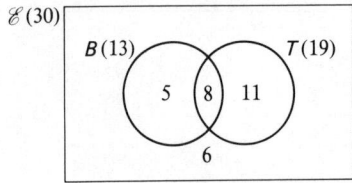

Figure L

Alternatively, of the 24 who play at least one game, 13 play basketball. Therefore, 11 play tennis only ($24 - 13 = 11$). As 19 people play tennis, 8 people play both games ($19 - 11 = 8$), and 5 play basketball only ($24 - 19 = 5$).

5   Let M = {houses that receive the *Daily Mirror*} and G = {houses that receive the *Guardian*}. See Figure M.

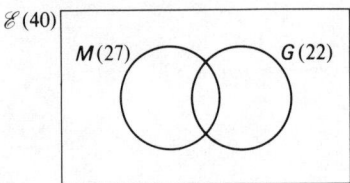

Figure M

(a) If every house has at least one paper, $n(M \cup G) = 40$, and so
$n(M \cap G) = 27 + 22 - 40 = 9$.

(b) There are fewer *Guardians* delivered than *Daily Mirrors*. So every house that has a *Guardian* could also have a *Daily Mirror* ($G \subset M$). In this case $n(M \cap G) = 22$.

4.4 Composite functions

 1 (a) See Figure N(a).
(b) 5 is the object. 13 is the image. 5 is mapped onto 13.
(c) The mapping *is* a function because for any particular object that you feed in, there is only one image.

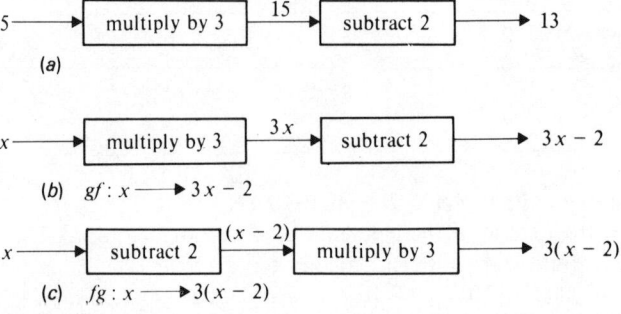

Figure N

68

2   The flow diagram for an object x is shown in Figure N(b).
    Hence $gf: x \to 3x-2$ or $gf(x) = 3x-2$.
3   (a) See Figure N(c). (b) $fg(5) = 3(5-2) = 9$ (c) $fg \neq gf$ (d) $fg: x \to 3(x-2)$
4   (a) 'divide by 3' (b) 'square' (c) See Figure O(a).
    (d) $h(9) = (9/3)^2 = 3^2 = 9$, $h(^-33) = (^-33/3)^2 = (^-11)^2 = {^+121}$
    (e) If $h = fg$, then $g: x \to x/3$ and $f: x \to x^2$.
    (Remember that $h = fg$ means that g is the first operation. From the flow diagram
    we see that the first operation is 'divide by 3'. f is the operation that follows
    g — 'square' from the flow diagram.)

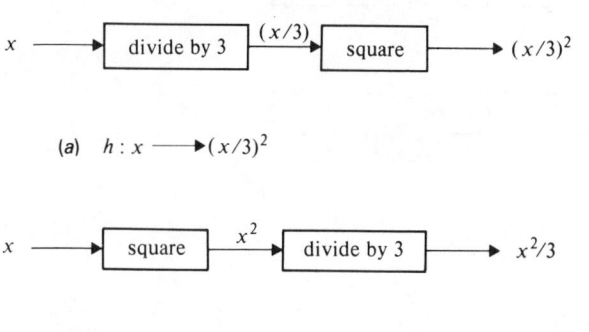

Figure O

5   (a) See Figure O(b).
    (b) $k(9) = (9^2)/3 = 81/3 = 27$, similarly $k(^-33) = 363$
    (c) $k: x \to (x^2)/3$ which is usually written $\frac{1}{3}x^2$.
6   (a) $1+3x = 1+(3x)$ (b) $2x^3 = 2(x^3)$ (c) $5/x-1 = (5/x)-1$

Exercise D

1   (a) $3-8 = {^-5}$ (b) $\frac{1}{4} \times 8 + 5 = 2+5 = 7$
    (c) $(5 \times 8+2)/6 = (40+2)/6 = 7$ (d) $30/(21-2 \times 8) = 30/(21-16) = 30/5 = 6$
    (e) $(^-2 \times 8+10)^2 = (^-16+10)^2 = (^-6)^2 = 36$
2   (a) $x \to x/4+3$ (b) $x \to x^2-5$ (c) $x \to 2(x+7)$
    (d) $x \to (x/2)^2$ (e) $x \to (x+3)^2/6$
3   (a) $q(7) = 14$, so $pq(7) = p(14) = 10$ (b) $pq(1) = {^-2}$
    (c) $p(7) = 3$, so $qp(7) = q(3) = 6$ (d) $qp(1) = {^-6}$
    $pq: x \to 2x-4$ and $qp: x \to 2(x-4)$
4   (a) $g(5) = 2\frac{1}{2}$, $fg(5) = f(2\frac{1}{2}) = 7\frac{1}{2}$ (b) $fg(^-4) = {^-6}$
    (c) $f(5) = 15$, $gf(5) = g(15) = 7\frac{1}{2}$ (d) $gf(^-4) = {^-6}$
    In this case, it appears that $fg = gf$. $fg: x \to 3(\frac{1}{2}x) = \frac{3}{2}x$ and $gf: x \to \frac{1}{2}(3x) = \frac{3}{2}x$,
    and so in this example fg and gf are in fact the same.
5   (a) $g: x \to 2x,$ $f: x \to x+3$
    (b) $g: x \to x-7,$ $f: x \to x^2$
    (c) $g: x \to 1/x,$ $f: x \to x+5$
    (d) $g: x \to x/3,$ $f: x \to 10-x$
    (e) $g: x \to x+30, f: x \to \sin x°$

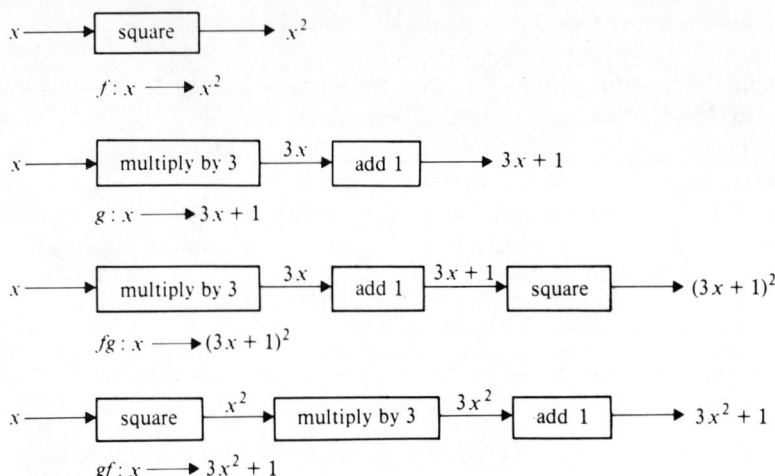

Figure P

6 See Figure P.
   (a) $fg(3) = 100$ and $gf(3) = 28$
   (b) $fg(-2) = 25$ and $gf(-2) = 13$
   (c) $fg(x) = (3x+1)^2$ and $gf(x) = 3x^2+1$

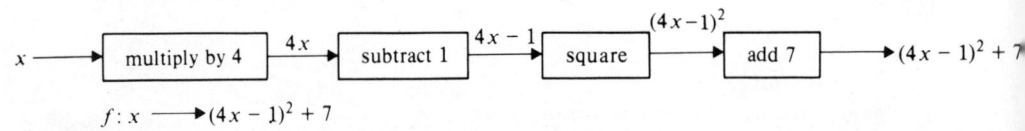

Figure Q

7 See Figure Q. If $f = pqrs$, s is 'multiply by 4' ($x \to 4x$), r is 'subtract 1' ($x \to x-1$), q is 'square' ($x \to x^2$), and p is 'add 7' ($x \to x+7$).

4.5 Inverses of composite functions

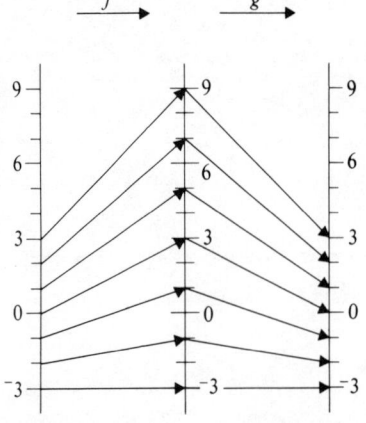

Figure R

1 (a) and (c). See Figure R.
   (b) The range of f (and the domain of g) is {−3, −1, 1, 3, 5, 7, 9}.
   (d) The range of g and the domain of f are the same. Hence, f and g are inverse functions, that is, g undoes the effect of f.

2 See Figure S.

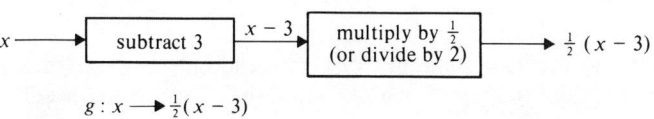

$g : x \rightarrow \tfrac{1}{2}(x-3)$

Figure S

3 It does not matter which letter we use in a flow diagram — it is a 'dummy', standing for any individual member of the domain.

Note that 'divide by 2' and 'multiply by $\tfrac{1}{2}$' are identical operations, and so $\dfrac{y-3}{2}$, $(y-3)/2$, $(y-3)\div 2$, and $\tfrac{1}{2}(y-3)$ are just different ways of writing the same thing.

Exercise E

1 (a) $x \rightarrow (x-5)/3$ (b) $x \rightarrow 5(x+2)$
   (c) $x \rightarrow \tfrac{1}{4}x - 7$ (d) $x \rightarrow \tfrac{1}{2}(5x-3)$
   (e) $x \rightarrow \pm\sqrt{[\tfrac{1}{2}(x-1)]}$ (f) $x \rightarrow 3 - x/6$
   (g) $x \rightarrow$ cube root of $10(x+7)$ (h) $x \rightarrow (x-3)^2$
   (i) $x \rightarrow 1 - \dfrac{1}{1-x}$

Figure T(a) shows the flow diagram for part (i). Since all these operations are self-inverse, we obtain the inverse flow diagram of Figure T(b). So this is a self-inverse composite function.

All these inverses are functions except (e).

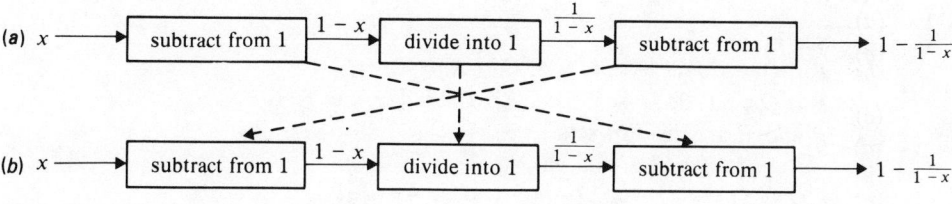

Figure T

2 (a) $f^{-1}: x \to x+3$ and $g^{-1}: x \to x/7$
   $f(5) = 2$, $g(5) = 35$, $fg(5) = 32$, $gf(5) = 14$, $f^{-1}(5) = 8$, $g^{-1}(5) = 5/7$,
   $(fg)^{-1}(5) = 8/7$, $(gf)^{-1}(5) = 26/7$, $f^{-1}g^{-1}(5) = 26/7$, $g^{-1}f^{-1}(5) = 8/7$
   Figure U(a) shows the flow diagram for fg, and Figure U(b) gives that of its inverse. From these we obtain $(fg)^{-1}(5) = 8/7$. $(gf)^{-1}(5)$ is worked out similarly. $f^{-1}g^{-1}(5)$ means $f^{-1}(g^{-1}(5))$, or $f^{-1}(5/7) = 5/7 + 3 = 26/7$.
   Similarly, $g^{-1}f^{-1}(5) = g^{-1}(8) = 8/7$.
(c) From these results and the flow diagrams for $(fg)^{-1}$ and $(gf)^{-1}$ we see that $(fg)^{-1}$ is f^{-1} followed by g^{-1} (that is, $(fg)^{-1} = g^{-1}f^{-1}$) and $(gf)^{-1}$ is g^{-1} followed by f^{-1} (that is, $(gf)^{-1} = f^{-1}g^{-1}$).

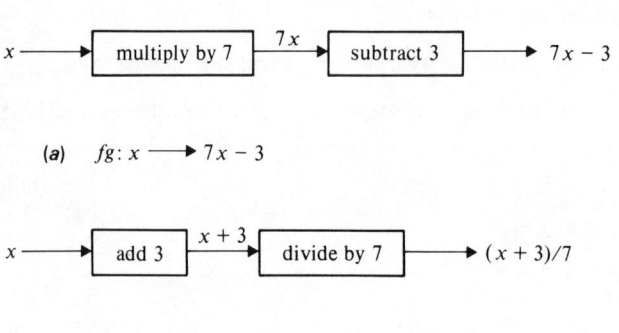

Figure U

Post-test

1 (a) See Figure V.
   (b) $P \cap Q = \{2, 4\}$, $P \cap R = \emptyset$, $Q \cap R = \{6, 8\}$,
       $P \cup Q = \{1, 2, 3, 4, 5, 6, 8\}$, $Q \cup R = \{2, 4, 6, 8, 10\}$
   (c) P and R are disjoint sets.
   (d) $n(P) = 5$, $n(P \cap R) = 0$, $n(Q \cup R) = 5$
   (e) $n(Q \cap S) = n(Q) + n(S) - n(Q \cup S) = 4 + 7 - 9 = 2$

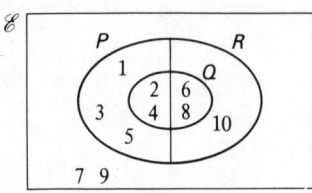

Figure V

2 (a) The flow diagram for the function f is shown in Figure W(a).
If $f = ghj$, then j is 'multiply by 4' or $x \rightarrow 4x$,
h is 'subtract 3' or $x \rightarrow x-3$,
and g is 'divide by 7' or $x \rightarrow x/7$.

(b) The inverse flow diagram for f is shown in Figure W(b).
$f^{-1}(3) = 6$, and $f^{-1}(x) = (7x+3)/4$ (or $\frac{1}{4}(7x+3)$)

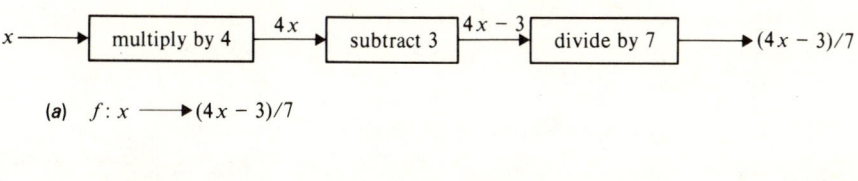

Figure W

3 (a) See Figure X.
(b) $f^{-1}: x \rightarrow (2x+4)/9$, $f(2) = 7$, $f^{-1}(7) = 2$, $f(-\frac{1}{2}) = -4\frac{1}{4}$, $f^{-1}(-4\frac{1}{4}) = -\frac{1}{2}$
If $f(x) = a$, then $x = f^{-1}(a)$,

because if $x \rightarrow a$, then $a \xrightarrow{f^{-1}} x$, that is, $f^{-1}: a \rightarrow x$ or $f^{-1}(a) = x$.
(c) If $f(x) = 7$, then $x = f^{-1}(7) = 2$.
(d) If $f(x) = -4\frac{1}{4}$, then $x = f^{-1}(-4\frac{1}{4}) = -\frac{1}{2}$.
(e) Hence, if $\frac{1}{2}(9x-4) = -6\frac{1}{2}$, then $f(x) = -6\frac{1}{2}$, and so $x = f^{-1}(-6\frac{1}{2}) = -1$.

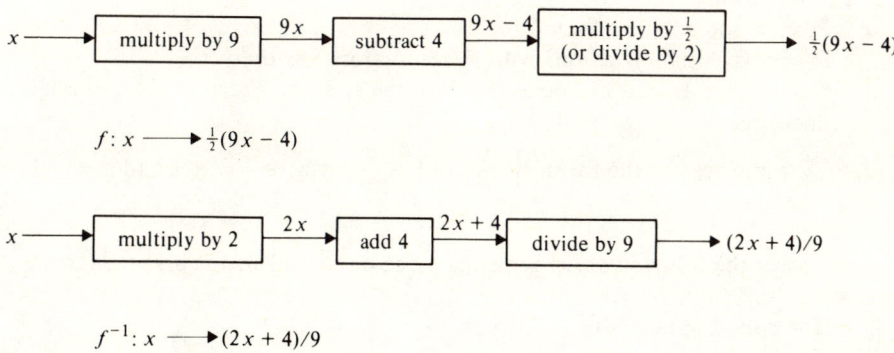

Figure X

5 Mathematical structure

Objectives

In this chapter we shall illustrate the place in the structure of mathematics of various topics that you have already met.
This is what you should be able to do after studying this chapter.
(1) Understand the mathematical meaning of the words element, operation and relation.
(2) Recognise when, for a given set of elements, an operation is commutative, and associative, and when the set is closed under the operation.
(3) Identify (where they exist) the identity element, and the inverse elements of a set, for a given operation.
(4) Use the distributive law for a given set and two operations.
(5) Understand and use the symbols $\Rightarrow$, $\Leftarrow$ and $\Leftrightarrow$.

Pre-test

1   List the following sets.
    (a) Positive integers less than 6
    (b) Proper (positive) fractions with denominators less than 5
    (c) Geometrical transformations in which the size and shape of the given figure is unchanged
    (d) 2×2 matrices of the form $\begin{bmatrix} p & 0 \\ 0 & q \end{bmatrix}$ or $\begin{bmatrix} 0 & p \\ q & 0 \end{bmatrix}$, where $p = \pm 1$ and $q = \pm 1$

2   Write down the following sets by listing three or four elements and then using dots...
    (a) The counting numbers
    (b) The integers
    (c) Quadrilaterals
    (d) Self-inverse functions

3   Draw a Venn diagram to show the sets $A = \{1, 2, 3\}$, $B = \{1, 3, 5\}$ and $C = \{1, 2, 4, 8\}$.
    List the elements of $A \cap B$ and $A \cup C$.

4 $G = \begin{bmatrix} 1 & 2 \\ -2 & 3 \end{bmatrix}$ and $H = \begin{bmatrix} 0 & -4 \\ -1 & 2 \end{bmatrix}$. Evaluate the following.
   (a) G+H   (b) H+G
   (c) G−H   (d) H−G
   (e) G H   (f) H G

5 *f* is the function 'divide by 4' and *g* is the function 'add 3'.
   (a) Express *f*, *g*, *fg* and *gf* in the form $f: x \to \ldots$
   (b) Evaluate $f(7)$, $g(7)$, $fg(7)$, $gf(7)$, $f^{-1}(7)$ and $g^{-1}(7)$.

5.1 Elements, operations and relations

Here are four mathematical 'statements'.
(a) $x + y = 5$
(b) $x \div \sqrt{} > \in {}^-3$
(c) $A \cap B \subset C$
(d) $(5 + 2x)/(5y - 1)$

1 One of these statements is nonsense. Which one?

2 One of these statements makes sense as far as it goes, but it is incomplete. Which one?

The other two make sense, and are complete. What do they have in common? Before we answer this question, we are going to look at the nature of the 'things' used in mathematics.
   There are three different types of 'things' used in these statements, namely
      (1) elements, such as *x*, *y*, 5, ⁻3, *A*, *B*, *C*
      (2) operations, such as +, ÷, ∩, √
   and (3) relations, such as =, >, ⊂, ∈
If we think of mathematics as a language, then the elements are the nouns, the operations are the conjunctions (much more important in mathematics), and the relations are the verbs. (The extras such as brackets are the punctuation.)
   You should now be able to see that (a) and (c) above are of the form element/operation/element/relation/element; in other words, they possess the same 'structure'. When we use a structure such as this we refer to it as *algebra*. If the elements are numbers (or symbols representing numbers), we call it *number algebra*. If the elements are vectors, it is called *vector algebra*.

3 What do we call the algebra whose elements are matrices?

Exercise A

1 Name some different kinds of numbers, other than integers, that are elements in number algebra.

2 What are the elements, operations and relations used in matrix algebra?

3 What are the elements used in transformation algebra? List four that you have met so far.

4 Name four of the operations used in number algebra.

5 The elements of set algebra are sets, including $\mathscr{E}$ and ø. Name two operations, and two relations, that are used in set algebra.

6 Relations such as equality, ordering, and so on, connect elements of a set or of two sets. (Note that the elements of this structure are the individual elements.)
(a) Draw the arrow diagram for the two sets $A = \{3, 4, 12\}$ and $B = \{2, 3, 4\}$ under the relation 'is greater than'.
(b) The arrows in Figure 1 define relations. State the relation in each case.

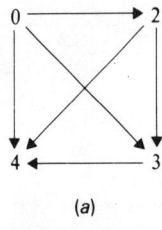
(a)

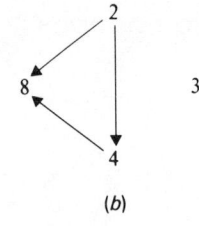
(b)

Figure 1

7 Make sensible mathematical statements out of the following by entering a suitable relation between each pair of elements.
(a) $2 \square 3$ (b) $\frac{7}{15} \square \frac{8}{17}$ (c) $\frac{9}{18} \square \frac{1}{2}$
(d) $\{1, 2, 3\} \square \{1, 2, 3, 4\}$ (e) $\{2, 5, \frac{1}{2}\} \square \{\frac{1}{2}, 2, 5\}$
(f) $\begin{bmatrix} 1 & 2 \\ 2 & -1 \end{bmatrix} \square \begin{bmatrix} 1 & 2 \\ 2 & -1 \end{bmatrix}$ (g) $\begin{bmatrix} 2 \\ 4 \end{bmatrix} \square \begin{bmatrix} -2 \\ -4 \end{bmatrix}$
(h) {factors of 12} $\square$ {factors of 24}

Operations

Mappings such as $x \rightarrow \sqrt{x}$ (take the square root),
$x \rightarrow 1/x$ (take the reciprocal),
and $P \rightarrow \mathbf{M}(P)$ (where $\mathbf{M}$ is a transformation)
are operations on one element only, and are sometimes called *unary operations*.

1 Write down two more unary operations.

Usually, however, we work with operations on two elements (as in statements (a) and (c) at the beginning of section 5.1). Such operations are called *binary operations*.
You have probably listed the basic four binary operations of arithmetic (addition, subtraction, multiplication, division) in answering question **4** of Exercise A.

2 Write down some binary operations that you have used when working with the following.
(a) Vectors (b) Matrices (c) Functions (d) Transformations (e) Sets

We often use symbols to represent operations. The symbols $+$, $-$, $\times$, $\div$ for the operations of arithmetic are universally understood. (However, it is necessary to remember that when used in matrix algebra or clock arithmetic they may not have their usual interpretations. To remind us of this, they are sometimes written in the form $\oplus$, $\otimes$, and so on. For example, in clock arithmetic modulo 7, $5 \oplus 4 = 2$.)

For other operations we use symbols such as $*$, $\circ$, $\#$, defining their meaning in each particular problem. Thus we might define $a \# b$ to be 'the highest common factor of a and b', or $a \circ b$ as 'the function b followed by the function a', or $a * b$ as 'the result of adding $2a$ to b'.

The most frequent operation in mathematics is that of multiplication in one form or another (including 'followed by' for functions and transformations), and so for this operation just a dot ., or sometimes nothing at all, is often used. For example, the product of two matrices **P** and **Q** may be written as $\mathbf{P} \times \mathbf{Q}$ or simply as **PQ**. (Mathematicians are inherently lazy, and want to write down as little as possible! So, since pq can stand for *one* operation on p and q without confusion, it is sensible to choose the one that is written down most often.) The exception to this convention is in the combination of numbers, because of our use of 'place value'. Thus, 23 means 'two tens and three' (not 2×3), and $5\frac{1}{4}$ means 'five plus one-quarter' (not $5 \times \frac{1}{4}$).

Exercise B

1. Enter a suitable operation between the two elements on the left-hand side of each of the following.
   (a) $2 \square 7 = 9$ (b) $3 \square 4 = 81$ (c) $\{a, b\} \square \{b\} = \{b\}$ (d) $\{a, b\} \square \{b\} = \{a, b\}$
   (e) $\begin{bmatrix} 1 & 2 \\ 3 & 4 \end{bmatrix} \square \begin{bmatrix} 3 & 4 \\ 5 & 6 \end{bmatrix} = \begin{bmatrix} -2 & -2 \\ -2 & -2 \end{bmatrix}$ (f) $\begin{bmatrix} 1 \\ 3 \end{bmatrix} \square \begin{bmatrix} -1 \\ -5 \end{bmatrix} = \begin{bmatrix} 2 \\ 8 \end{bmatrix}$
   (g) $101_2 \square 11_2 = 1000_2$ (h) $23_9 \square 3_9 = 7_9$

2. The operation $*$ means 'add twice the first number to half the second number' (for example, $2 * 6 = 4 + 3 = 7$). Calculate the values of these.
   (a) $1 * 2$ (b) $3 * 4$ (c) $4 * 3$
   (d) $0 * 2$ (e) $2 * 0$ (f) $0 * 0$
   Is it true that $a * b = b * a$ for all values of a and b?

3. The operation $\#$ is defined by $a \# b = a^2 b$ (for example, $3 \# 4 = 36$). Find the values of (a) to (j).
   (a) $1 \# 2$ (b) $2 \# 1$ (c) $0 \# 4$ (d) $4 \# 0$
   (e) $(2 \# 1) \# 2$ (f) $2 \# (1 \# 2)$ (g) $^-1 \# 3$
   (h) $3 \# ^-1$ (i) $(^-1 \# 3) \# 2$ (j) $^-1 \# (3 \# 2)$
   (k) Is $a \# b$ always the same as $b \# a$?
   (l) Is $(a \# b) \# c$ always the same as $a \# (b \# c)$?

4. (a) If $f: x \to 2x$ and $g: x \to x+1$, express fg and gf in the forms $fg: x \to \ldots$ and $gf: x \to \ldots$
   (b) What binary operation is used here?
   (c) What are the elements in this algebra?

5.2 Commutativity, associativity and closure

Commutativity and rearrangement

In questions **2** and **3** of Exercise B you will have noticed that $a*b$ was not always the same as $b*a$, and $a \# b$ was not always the same as $b \# a$ for the operations defined in those questions.

▷ 1 Calculate these. (a) $\begin{bmatrix} 1 & 2 \\ 3 & 4 \end{bmatrix} \begin{bmatrix} 5 & 6 \\ 7 & 8 \end{bmatrix}$ and $\begin{bmatrix} 5 & 6 \\ 7 & 8 \end{bmatrix} \begin{bmatrix} 1 & 2 \\ 3 & 4 \end{bmatrix}$

(b) $\begin{bmatrix} 1 & 2 \\ 3 & 4 \end{bmatrix} + \begin{bmatrix} 5 & 6 \\ 7 & 8 \end{bmatrix}$ and $\begin{bmatrix} 5 & 6 \\ 7 & 8 \end{bmatrix} + \begin{bmatrix} 1 & 2 \\ 3 & 4 \end{bmatrix}$

Your answer for 1(a) should remind you that for matrix multiplication the order in which the matrices are written down can affect the answer. However, answer 1(b) suggests that for matrix addition the order does not matter.

2 Complete the following statements with either = or ≠.
(a) $4+3 \square 3+4$ (b) $4-3 \square 3-4$ (c) $2^3 \square 3^2$
(d) $5 \times 6 \square 6 \times 5$ (e) $5 \div 6 \square 6 \div 5$
(f) $A \cap B \square B \cap A$ (g) $A \cup B \square B \cup A$
(h) $[x \to 3x+2$ followed by $x \to 2x] \square [x \to 2x$ followed by $x \to 3x+2]$

These are all questions about the *commutativity* of the operation. We say that the operation is commutative if it does not matter in which order the elements are combined. Thus the operations of + and × on the set of real numbers are commutative, but the operations of − and ÷ are not.

More formally, any operation denoted by * is said to be *commutative* on a set S if $a*b = b*a$ for all elements a, b of S.

It is not sufficient for $a*b$ to equal $b*a$ for *some* values of a and b. For commutativity this must be true for *all* values of a and b of the set S. For example, $4^2 = 2^4$, but in general $a^b \neq b^a$, and so this operation is not commutative.

Exercise C

▷ 1 State whether the operations defined for the sets below are commutative.

	Elements	Operation
(a)	Rotations in the plane about the origin	'followed by'
(b)	Quarter-turns about any point in the plane	'followed by'
(c)	Reflections in lines through the origin	'followed by'
(d)	3×2 matrices	subtraction
(e)	Positive integers	'take the highest common factor'
(f)	Positive integers	'find the difference between'

2 (a) Is $8-3$ the same as $3-8$? Is it the same as $^-3+8$?
   (b) Is $15-23$ the same as $23-15$? Is it the same as $^-23+15$?

78

Associativity

In question **3** of Exercise B we calculated (2 # 1) # 2 and 2 # (1 # 2), and decided that for the operation #, (a # b) # c is not always the same as a # (b # c).

1 Work out each of these.
(a) 4 + (5 + 6) and (4 + 5) + 6
(b) 3 × (2 × 4) and (3 × 2) × 4
(c) 36 ÷ (6 ÷ 3) and (36 ÷ 6) ÷ 3
(d) $(3^4)^2$ and $3^{(4^2)}$ (Express each as a single power of 3.)
(e) $\left(\begin{bmatrix} 2 & 1 \\ 1 & 3 \end{bmatrix}\begin{bmatrix} -1 & 0 \\ 2 & 4 \end{bmatrix}\right)\begin{bmatrix} 3 & 4 \\ 6 & 7 \end{bmatrix}$ and $\begin{bmatrix} 2 & 1 \\ 1 & 3 \end{bmatrix}\left(\begin{bmatrix} -1 & 0 \\ 2 & 4 \end{bmatrix}\begin{bmatrix} 3 & 4 \\ 6 & 7 \end{bmatrix}\right)$

2 (a) Draw two Venn diagrams as in Figure 2. In one, shade (A ∩ B) ∩ C, and in the other A ∩ (B ∩ C). Are they the same?
(b) Is (A ∪ B) ∪ C the same as A ∪ (B ∪ C)?

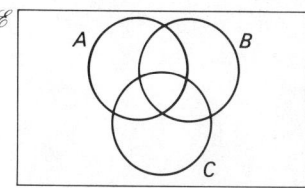

Figure 2

If (a * b) * c does equal a * (b * c) for all values of a, b and c, then we say that the operation is *associative*. In such cases we may leave out the brackets and write a * b * c without confusion. If the operation is not associative (as in question **3** of Exercise B, and division on the set of real numbers), then brackets should be used to make clear in which order the operations are to be applied, In practice, if no brackets are present, expressions such as 43 − 15 − 22 are worked from left to right (this one becomes 28 − 22 = 6).

3 Work out, by this convention, (a) 36 ÷ 4 ÷ 3 and (b) 45 − 17 + 6.

Formally, any operation denoted by * is said to be *associative* over a set S if (a * b) * c = a * (b * c) for all elements a, b, c of the set S.

As with commutativity and the other properties that we shall meet later in this chapter, if we can find one example for which the property does not hold, then the operation does not have that property. In theory, to prove that the property does hold for a particular set we ought to try it for all possible combinations of the elements of that set. This is usually not possible (especially if the set is infinite in size!), but in most cases we are able to make a sensible deduction after looking at a few examples.

Here is a guide to operations that are associative.
(1) Most operations involving addition or multiplication (for example, addition and multiplication of matrices) are associative.
(2) (as a special case of (1)) 'followed by' for transformations and functions is associative.
(3) Union and intersection of sets are associative.

Closure

If we consider the operation ÷ on the set of positive integers, we find that sometimes the combination of two elements gives a result that does not belong to the set (of positive integers). For example, 18÷4 gives $4\frac{1}{2}$, which is not an integer. In this case we say that the set of positive integers is not *closed* under the operation of division.

1. (a) Is the set of positive rational numbers (numbers of the form p/q, where p and q are integers – in other words, fractions) closed under division?
   (b) Is the set of positive integers closed under multiplication?

Formally, a set S is said to be *closed* under an operation $*$ if, for all a, b belonging to S, the result of $a*b$ is also a member of S.

Exercise D

1. $a*b$ is defined as $a+2b$, where a and b are real numbers.
   (a) Work these out. $(1*2)*3$ and $1*(2*3)$, $(p*q)*r$ and $p*(q*r)$
   (b) Is this operation commutative or associative?
   (c) Is the set of real numbers closed under this operation?

2. **p** and **q** are vectors, and the operation $*$ on them is defined by

$$\mathbf{p}*\mathbf{q} = \mathbf{p} + \tfrac{1}{2}\mathbf{q}.$$

If $\mathbf{p} = \begin{bmatrix} -1 \\ 2 \end{bmatrix}$, $\mathbf{q} = \begin{bmatrix} 3 \\ 2 \end{bmatrix}$ and $\mathbf{r} = \begin{bmatrix} 2 \\ 3 \end{bmatrix}$, calculate these.

(a) $\mathbf{p}*\mathbf{q}$ (b) $\mathbf{q}*\mathbf{p}$ (c) $\mathbf{q}*\mathbf{r}$ (d) $(\mathbf{p}*\mathbf{q})*\mathbf{r}$ (e) $\mathbf{p}*(\mathbf{q}*\mathbf{r})$

What can you say about the operation $*$?

5.3 Identity and inverse elements

The identity element

1. A and B are any non-empty sets. Simplify the following.
   (a) $A \cup \emptyset$ and $\emptyset \cup A$ (b) $\emptyset \cup B$ and $B \cup \emptyset$ (c) $\mathscr{E} \cap A$ and $A \cap \mathscr{E}$
   (d) $B \cap \mathscr{E}$ and $\mathscr{E} \cap B$

2. Evaluate the following.

   (a) $\begin{bmatrix} 1 & 0 \\ 0 & 1 \end{bmatrix} \begin{bmatrix} 3 & 2 \\ 1 & 1 \end{bmatrix}$ and $\begin{bmatrix} 3 & 2 \\ 1 & 1 \end{bmatrix} \begin{bmatrix} 1 & 0 \\ 0 & 1 \end{bmatrix}$

   (b) $\begin{bmatrix} 1 & 0 \\ 0 & 1 \end{bmatrix} \begin{bmatrix} 0 & 3 \\ 3 & 0 \end{bmatrix}$ and $\begin{bmatrix} 0 & 3 \\ 3 & 0 \end{bmatrix} \begin{bmatrix} 1 & 0 \\ 0 & 1 \end{bmatrix}$

   (c) $\begin{bmatrix} 1 & 2 & 3 \\ 4 & 5 & 6 \end{bmatrix} + \begin{bmatrix} 0 & 0 & 0 \\ 0 & 0 & 0 \end{bmatrix}$ and $\begin{bmatrix} 0 & 0 & 0 \\ 0 & 0 & 0 \end{bmatrix} + \begin{bmatrix} 1 & 2 & 3 \\ 4 & 5 & 6 \end{bmatrix}$

   (d) $\begin{bmatrix} -2 \\ 4 \\ 16 \end{bmatrix} + \begin{bmatrix} 0 \\ 0 \\ 0 \end{bmatrix}$ and $\begin{bmatrix} 0 \\ 0 \\ 0 \end{bmatrix} + \begin{bmatrix} -2 \\ 4 \\ 16 \end{bmatrix}$

In each case, any randomly chosen element of the set is unchanged when combined with a certain element from that set. This special element is different for different operations on a set. For sets under the operation of union, this special element is ø.

For 2×2 matrices under the operation of multiplication it is $\begin{bmatrix} 1 & 0 \\ 0 & 1 \end{bmatrix}$.

For 2×3 matrices under addition it is $\begin{bmatrix} 0 & 0 & 0 \\ 0 & 0 & 0 \end{bmatrix}$.

We call this special element the *identity element* of the set for the given operation. Its special feature is that when it is combined with any other element of the set, that other element is unaltered.

For example, the identity element for the set of real numbers under addition is 0, because $x + 0 = x$ (so x is unchanged) whichever number is substituted for x.

3 What is the identity for the set of real numbers under multiplication?

Formally, the element e of a set S is the identity element of that set under an operation $*$ if
$$a * e = e * a = a, \text{ for all } a \text{ belonging to } S.$$

Note that for e to be a 'true' identity, the result must be true whichever way round the elements are combined.

4 If x is a real number, does $x - 0 = x$? Does $0 - x = x$? Is there a 'true' identity for numbers under subtraction?

5 If $*$ stands for the operation 'take the highest common factor of' on the set of positive integers, work out the following.
(a) $1 * 6$ (b) $6 * 1$ (c) $35 * 1$ (d) $1 * 128$
(e) $36 * 42$ (f) $125 * 216$ (g) $48 * 48$
Is there an identity element for this operation?

Although identity elements do not always exist, note that it is still possible for an operation to be non-commutative and yet have an identity, as in the multiplication of matrices. If the operation is a type of addition, the identity element is sometimes called the *zero* element. For multiplication-type operations, the identity is sometimes called the *unit* element. On the whole, the single term *identity* is to be preferred, whatever the operation.

Inverse elements

1 Work out the following.

(a) $\begin{bmatrix} 3 & 2 \\ 1 & 1 \end{bmatrix} \begin{bmatrix} 1 & -2 \\ -1 & 3 \end{bmatrix}$ and $\begin{bmatrix} 1 & -2 \\ -1 & 3 \end{bmatrix} \begin{bmatrix} 3 & 2 \\ 1 & 1 \end{bmatrix}$

(b) $\begin{bmatrix} -4 & -5 \\ 1 & 1 \end{bmatrix} \begin{bmatrix} 1 & 5 \\ -1 & -4 \end{bmatrix}$ and $\begin{bmatrix} 1 & 5 \\ -1 & -4 \end{bmatrix} \begin{bmatrix} -4 & -5 \\ 1 & 1 \end{bmatrix}$

When combining 2×2 matrices by multiplication, it is sometimes possible to find a pair **A** and **B** such that

$$\mathbf{AB} = \mathbf{BA} = \begin{bmatrix} 1 & 0 \\ 0 & 1 \end{bmatrix} \quad \text{(the identity matrix)}.$$

When this is so, we say that **B** is the *inverse* of **A** (written as $\mathbf{B} = \mathbf{A}^{-1}$), **A** is the *inverse* of **B** ($\mathbf{A} = \mathbf{B}^{-1}$), and that **A** and **B** are an *inverse pair*.

2. In Chapter 4, we considered the inverses of functions.
   (a) What are the inverses of these functions? $f: x \to 3x$, $g: x \to x-10$
   (b) What is the result of applying $f^{-1}f$ to x?
   (c) What is the result of applying ff^{-1} to x?

   Again, for S, the set of integers under addition, given an element of S (say $^+7$), we can find another element of S which has the opposite effect ($^-7$ in this case). Here

   $$^-7 + {^+7} = 0, \text{ the identity element.}$$

   So, for an operation $*$, we can sometimes find an element q that 'counteracts' the element p. Then $q*p$ is equal to the identity element under $*$.

   In such cases we say that the element q is the inverse of p. Sometimes we write $q = p^{-1}$, so that for the example above we could write

   $$\text{under addition, } 7^{-1} = {^-7}.$$

   (This would be read as 'under addition, the inverse of 7 is negative 7.)

3. Suppose we now consider the set of all real numbers under multiplication.
   (a) What is the identity element now?
   (b) What is the inverse of 7 now?
   (c) What is the inverse of $\frac{1}{2}$?
   (d) Which number has no (finite) inverse under multiplication?

   So we can write
   $$\text{under multiplication, } 7^{-1} = \tfrac{1}{7}.$$

   In practice, the convention for numbers (and letters that are standing for numbers) is that, unless another operation is specifically stated, n^{-1} means the inverse of n under multiplication,

   $$\text{that is, } n^{-1} = \frac{1}{n} \text{ (the reciprocal of } n\text{).}$$

   (Remember that if no operation is stated in the combination pq, it is understood that multiplication is involved: $pq = p \times q$.)

   Formally, for a set S under an operation $*$, a and b are an inverse pair of elements of S if $a*b = b*a = e$, where e is the identity element of S under the operation $*$.

   If a set does possess an identity, there is only one identity element for the whole set. But when it comes to looking for inverses, remember that *each* element of the set may have an inverse, so that there may be several, or many, different inverse pairs in the set.

Exercise E

1. Write down the following for 2×2 matrices under the operation of addition.
   (a) The identity element
   (b) The inverses of $\begin{bmatrix} 1 & 2 \\ -3 & -4 \end{bmatrix}$ and $\begin{bmatrix} 4 & -5 \\ -6 & 0 \end{bmatrix}$
   (c) The element for which $\begin{bmatrix} 0 & -1 \\ 3 & -2 \end{bmatrix}$ is the inverse

2   The set *S* has four elements which are the transformations

   I = rotation of 0° about *O*,
   H = a half-turn about *O*,
   P = reflection in *WX*,
   Q = reflection in *YZ*,

on the rectangle *ABCD* (see Figure 3). The operation ∗ is 'followed by' (using the convention that **H** ∗ **P** means **P** followed by **H**).

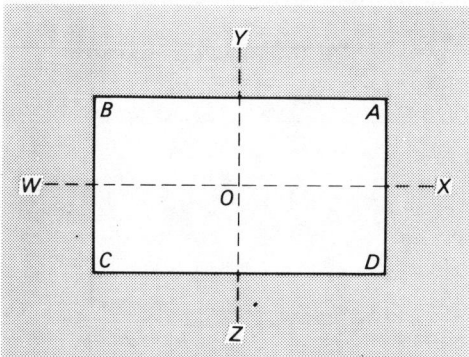

Figure 3

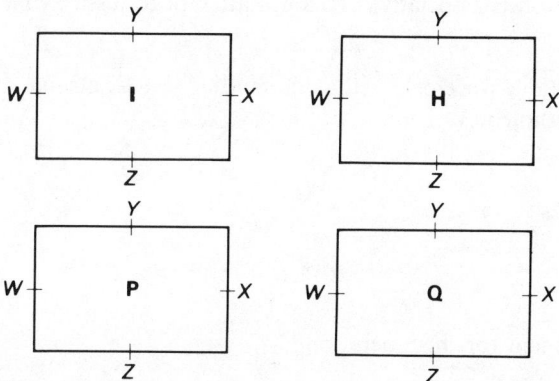

Figure 4

(a) Copy Figure 4 and label the corners to show the positions of *A, B, C* and *D* after each of the four transformations.
(b) Which is the identity element?
(c) Show that **P** ∗ **H** is equivalent to **Q**.
   Simplify **H** ∗ **P**, **H** ∗ **Q**, **Q** ∗ **H** and **P** ∗ **P** in the same way.
(d) What are the inverses of **H** and **P**?
(e) Complete the combination table shown. (**P** ∗ **H** = **Q** is entered to remind you that the element at the side is that *written down* first.)

∗	I	H	P	Q
I				
H				
P		Q		
Q				

(f) Is this operation commutative?

83

(The ideas in this question can be compared to putting a rectangular piece of frosted glass into a window frame. In answering this question you may find it helpful to cut out, from a piece of thin card, a rectangle of the same size as *ABCD*, and label it 'front' and 'back', and letter the four corners on both sides. For the purposes of this question, reflection in *WX* is equivalent to turning the cardboard over about the axis *WX*; i.e. a three-dimensional half-turn about *WX*. Similarly for **Q**.)

3 When the elements are functions, the operation is 'followed by' (with the same conventions as in question **2**).

(a) Copy and complete the combination table for the functions shown.

'followed by'	$x \to \tfrac{1}{2}x$	$x \to x$	$x \to 2x$	$x \to 2/x$
$x \to \tfrac{1}{2}x$	$x \to \tfrac{1}{4}x$	$x \to \tfrac{1}{2}x$	$x \to x$	$x \to 1/x$
$x \to x$				
$x \to 2x$				
$x \to 2/x$				

(b) Which is the identity element?
(c) Write down the inverses of $x \to 2x$ and $x \to 2/x$.
(d) Is the set closed under this operation?
(e) Is the operation commutative?
(f) Do you think the operation is associative? (Do not attempt to justify your guess!)

4 (a) Copy and complete this table for clock arithmetic modulo 4. ($+_4$ means addition in modulo 4 arithmetic.)

$+_4$	0	1	2	3
0	0	1		
1				
2				
3			1	2

(b) Which is the identity element for this operation?
(c) Which element is the inverse of 2?
(d) Which element is the inverse of 3?
(e) Is the set {0, 1, 2, 3} closed under this operation?
(f) Is this operation commutative?
(g) Do you think this operation is associative?

5 Here is an unfinished table for multiplication in modulo 4 arithmetic (denoted by $\times_4$). Repeat question **4** for this operation.

$\times_4$	0	1	2	3
0				
1				
2	0	2	0	2
3				

84

5.4 The distributive law, and further developments

The distributive law

1. Work out the following.
   (a) $3 \times (8+18)$
   (b) $(3 \times 8) + (3 \times 18)$
   (c) $3 + (8 \times 18)$
   (d) $(3+8) \times (3+18)$

2. Which of these results are the same? Would this still be true if the numbers 3, 8 and 18 were replaced by other numbers?

This suggests that, if p, q and r belong to the set of real numbers, then
$$p \times (q+r) = p \times q + p \times r, \text{ for all values of } p, q \text{ and } r.$$
This is the distributive law for multiplication over addition on the set of real numbers.

Conversely, we see that, for example, $9 \times 4 + 9 \times 7 = 9 \times (4+7)$, and in general $xy + xz = x(y+z)$. If we use the distributive law this way round we say that we have 'factorised' the expression.

3. (a) Make two copies of Figure 5. On one shade A, and on the other shade $B \cup C$.
   (b) On another copy of Figure 5, shade $A \cap (B \cup C)$.
   (c) Make two more copies of Figure 5 to show $A \cap B$ and $A \cap C$.
   (d) Hence show $(A \cap B) \cup (A \cap C)$.

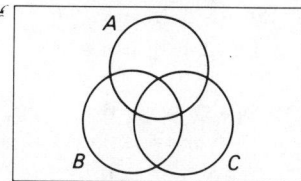

Figure 5

4. Is $A \cap (B \cup C)$ the same as $(A \cap B) \cup (A \cap C)$? Is the operation $\cap$ distributive over the operation $\cup$ for sets?

The use of the implication sign

If we know that $3x = 12$, it follows that $x = 4$. To save writing 'it follows that', we can use the *implication sign* like this
$$[3x = 12] \Rightarrow [x = 4],$$
or (using two lines) like this
$$3x = 12$$
$$\Rightarrow x = 4.$$
This is read as '$3x = 12$ implies that $x = 4$'.

In this example it is also true that if $x = 4$ then $3x = 12$. Thus we could also write
$$[x = 4] \Rightarrow [3x = 12], \text{ or } [3x = 12] \Leftarrow [x = 4].$$
(The latter form would be read as '$3x = 12$ is implied by $x = 4$'.)

In this particular case the implication is true both ways. If we know that either of the statements is true, then the other one is true also. So the two ideas can be combined by using the symbol ⇔.

$$[x = 4] \Leftrightarrow [3x = 12].$$

(This is sometimes read as '$x = 4$ if, and only if, $3x = 12$'.)

1 Is ⇒ an element, an operation, a relation, or punctuation?
2 (a) Is it true that $[x = 3] \Rightarrow [x^2 = 9]$?
   (b) Why is it not true to say that $[x^2 = 9] \Rightarrow [x = 3]$?

Further developments

We have now covered all the 'structure' that we need for the course, for which most of you will be thankful! However, some of you may be wondering where all this leads. If you do study mathematical structure any further, the next two stages are as follows.

(1) The justification of our methods for solving equations, using the structure ideas, and the axiom (assumption) that

$$[x = y] \Leftrightarrow [k * x = k * y],$$

where * may stand for addition, or multiplication provided $k \neq 0$.

We can give an idea of this in solving the equation $\quad 5(n+1) = n$.
Apply the distributive law $\qquad\qquad\qquad\qquad\qquad\qquad 5n + 5 = n$
Add ^-n (the inverse of n under $+$) to both sides $\qquad (5n + 5) + {^-n} = n + {^-n}$
Apply the associative law $\qquad\qquad\qquad\qquad\qquad\quad 5n + 5 + {^-n} = n + {^-n}$
(element + inverse = identity) $\qquad\qquad\qquad\qquad\qquad\qquad = 0$
Apply the commutative law $\qquad\qquad\qquad\qquad\qquad\; 5n + {^-n} + 5 = 0$
$\qquad\qquad\qquad\qquad\qquad\qquad\qquad\qquad\qquad\qquad\quad 4n + 5 = 0$
Add $^-5$ (the inverse of 5 under $+$) to both sides $\qquad (4n + 5) + {^-5} = 0 + {^-5}$
Apply associative, commutative and identity
  ideas as before $\qquad\qquad\qquad\qquad\qquad\qquad\qquad\qquad 4n + 0 = {^-5}$
Multiply both sides by $\frac{1}{4}$
  (the inverse of 4 under $\times$) $\qquad\qquad\qquad\qquad\; \frac{1}{4} \times (4n) = \frac{1}{4} \times {^-5}$
Apply associative and identity ideas as before $\qquad\qquad 1 \times n = {^-\frac{5}{4}}$
So $\qquad\qquad\qquad\qquad\qquad\qquad\qquad\qquad\qquad\qquad\quad n = -1\frac{1}{4}$

In practice, of course, we apply many of these ideas automatically!

(2) The definition of a *group*. This is a set S of elements under an operation *, which obeys certain rules. The operation must be associative, the set must be closed under the operation and have an identity, and all the elements must have a unique inverse.

In a group, every equation has a unique solution.
Some examples of groups are:
  The set of real numbers under addition
  The set of real numbers, excluding zero, under multiplication
  Clock arithmetic modulo 5 under addition
  Clock arithmetic modulo 5 (except zero) under multiplication

The set of all rotations about the origin under 'followed by'
The symmetries of a rectangle (Exercise E, question 2)

Exercise F

1. $3(7+11) = 3 \times 7 + 3 \times 11 = 21 + 33$
   Work out the following in a similar way.
   (a) $5(10+11)$ (b) $4(a+b)$ (c) $x(5+4)$
   (d) $x(5+x)$ (e) $(x+y)5$ (f) $2(10+4b)$
   (g) $(4-x)x$ (h) $(8b+1)b$

2. Use the distributive law to rearrange the following. A, B and C are sets.
   (a) $A \cup (B \cap C)$ (b) $A \cap (B \cup C)$ (c) $(A \cap B) \cup C$
   (d) $(A \cup B) \cap C$

3. Factorise the following.
   (a) $3a+3b$ (b) $5a+6a$ (c) $3a+6b$ (d) $x+ax$
   (e) $8+4b$ (f) $ab+ac$ (g) $9x-x^2$ (h) $4x-2x^2$

4. Insert in the following the most appropriate sign from $\Rightarrow$, $\Leftarrow$ or $\Leftrightarrow$.
   (a) $[x > 4] \square [x = 5]$
   (b) [Martin is Joy's brother] $\square$ [Joy is Martin's sister]
   (c) [x is the son of y] $\square$ [y is the parent of x]
   (d) $[(x+4)(x-3) = 0] \square [x = 3]$
   (e) [x is greater than y and y is greater than z] $\square$ [x is greater than z]

Summary

(1) An element is one of the things used in mathematics. Examples of elements are numbers, matrices, sets, functions.

(2) A binary operation is a means of combining two elements. Examples of operations are addition, multiplication, intersection, 'followed by'.
   An operation is always defined in connection with a set of elements, as in addition with numbers, matrices under multiplication, transformations under 'followed by'.
   A unary operation acts upon one element only – for example, square root.

(3) A relation (for example, $=$, $>$, $\subset$) expresses a connection between two elements, such as $A \subset B$, $44 > 12$, $(2x-3) = 14$.

(4) An operation $*$ on a set S is said to be commutative if

$$a * b = b * a \quad \text{for all } a \text{ and } b \text{ belonging to } S.$$

The integers are commutative under addition.

(5) The operation $*$ on a set S is said to be associative if

$$(a * b) * c = a * (b * c) \quad \text{for all } a, b \text{ and } c \text{ belonging to } S.$$

The integers are associative under multiplication.

(6) The identity element e for a set S under the operation $*$ obeys the law

$$a*e = e*a = a \quad \text{for all } a \text{ belonging to } S.$$

For the integers under addition, the identity is 0 (sometimes called the zero element), and under multiplication it is 1 (sometimes called the unit element).

(7) If a is a member of S, the inverse (if it exists) of a under the operation $*$ is the element b, also belonging to S, such that

$$a*b = b*a = e, \text{ where } e \text{ is the identity of } S \text{ for the operation } *.$$

The inverse of a is often written as a^{-1}; that is $b = a^{-1}$.

For integers under addition, the inverse of 4 is $^-4$, the inverse of $^-6$ is $^+6$, and so on. Under multiplication, the inverse of 4 is $\frac{1}{4}$, the inverse of $^-5$ is $-\frac{1}{5}$, the inverse of $\frac{1}{2}$ is 2, and so on.

(8) A set S is closed under the operation $*$ if, for all a and b belonging to S, the combination of a and b, $a*b$, is also a member of S.

The set of positive integers is closed under multiplication, but not under division.

(9) The distributive law: Multiplication is distributive over addition for the set of real numbers, because

$$a \times (b+c) = a \times b + a \times c, \quad \text{for all } a, b \text{ and } c \text{ belonging to the set of real numbers.}$$

(10) $P \Rightarrow Q$ is read as 'P implies Q', meaning that if the statement P is true, then so is the statement Q. For example, $[x = 4] \Rightarrow [x^2 = 16]$. (Note that $[x^2 = 16] \not\Rightarrow [x = 4]$.)
$P \Leftarrow Q$ is equivalent to $Q \Rightarrow P$.
$a \in S \Leftarrow \{\text{vowels}\} \subset S$.
$P \Leftrightarrow Q$ means that $P \Rightarrow Q$ and $Q \Rightarrow P$; that is, if either of P or Q is a correct statement, then the other one is correct as well.

Post-test

1 List the elements, operations, relations and punctuation in the statement

$$[3(x+1) = 7] \Rightarrow [x > 1].$$

2 I is the set of positive integers. Give examples to show that the following statements are true.
   (a) Subtraction is not commutative over I.
   (b) Subtraction is not associative over I.
   (c) The set I is not closed under subtraction.

3 (a) Work out the combination table for multiplication modulo 12 ($\times_{12}$) for each of these sets.

$$A = \{1, 2\}, \quad B = \{4, 8\}, \quad C = \{2, 4, 8\}, \quad D = \{1, 5, 7, 11\}$$

   (b) Which sets are closed under this operation?
   (c) Give the identity element (if there is one) for each set.
   (d) List the inverses (if any) of the elements of each set.
   (e) Are any of the sets groups?

4   (a) Evaluate $\sqrt{9}$, $\sqrt{16}$, $\sqrt{(9+16)}$, $\sqrt{(9 \times 16)}$.
    (b) Use your results to decide whether $\sqrt{}$ is distributive over addition.
    (c) Is $\sqrt{}$ distributive over multiplication?

Assignment

1 The operation $*$ is defined on the set {2, 4, 6, 8} by the relation

$$a * b = \text{the unit digit in the product } a \times b.$$

   (a) Construct a table that shows the values of $a * b$ for all pairs of members of the set.
   (b) Is the operation commutative?
   (c) Is the operation associative?
   (d) Is the set closed under $*$?
   (e) What is the identity element?
   (f) Where possible, write down the inverse of each element.

2 The operation $\#$ is defined on the set of positive integers by

$$a \# b = \text{the highest common factor of } a \text{ and } b.$$

Work these out. (a) $4 \# 4$ (b) $6 \# 8$ (c) $30 \# (12 \# 9)$ (d) $(30 \# 12) \# 9$
(e) Find values of a, b and c such that

$$a \# (b+c) \neq a \# b + a \# c.$$

(f) Prove that

   [x is a factor of a and b and c] $\Leftrightarrow$ [x is a factor of $a \# (b \# c)$].

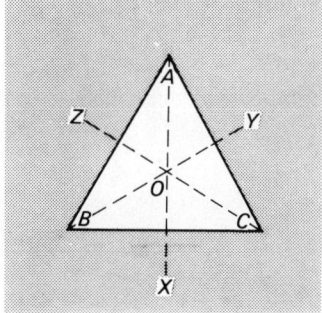

Figure 6

3 The set S has six elements, which are transformations on the equilateral triangle ABC (see Figure 6). These transformations are
   I = rotation of 0° about O,
   J = anticlockwise rotation of 120° about O,
   K = anticlockwise rotation of 240° about O,
   L = reflection in the line AX,
   M = reflection in the line BY,
   N = reflection in the line CZ.

(a) Draw six diagrams to show the position of the corners of the triangle after each of the transformations.
(b) Show that **K** * **L** = **M**, and that **N** * **J** = **L**.
(* is 'followed by'. **K** * **L** means **L** followed by **K**.)
(c) Which is the identity?
(d) Simplify **J** * **J**, **J** * **M**, **M** * **K** and **L** * **L**.
(e) What are the inverses of **J** and **M**?
(f) Compile the combination table.
(g) Is the operation closed?
(h) Is the operation associative?
(i) Is the operation commutative?
(Compare this set with that of question **2**, Exercise E.)

Answers

Pre-test

1 (a) {1, 2, 3, 4, 5} (b) {$\frac{1}{2}$, $\frac{1}{3}$, $\frac{2}{3}$, $\frac{1}{4}$, $\frac{3}{4}$} (in any order)
($\frac{2}{4}$ has not been included, as it is equal to $\frac{1}{2}$: some purists might regard $\frac{1}{2}$ and $\frac{2}{4}$ as 'equivalent' fractions, but nevertheless not the same fractions. They should include $\frac{2}{4}$ in the set!)
(c) {translation, reflection, rotation, glide reflection}
(d) $\left\{\begin{bmatrix}1 & 0\\0 & 1\end{bmatrix}, \begin{bmatrix}1 & 0\\0 & -1\end{bmatrix}, \begin{bmatrix}-1 & 0\\0 & 1\end{bmatrix}, \begin{bmatrix}-1 & 0\\0 & -1\end{bmatrix}, \begin{bmatrix}0 & 1\\1 & 0\end{bmatrix},\right.$
$\left.\begin{bmatrix}0 & -1\\1 & 0\end{bmatrix}, \begin{bmatrix}0 & 1\\-1 & 0\end{bmatrix}, \begin{bmatrix}0 & -1\\-1 & 0\end{bmatrix}\right\}$

2 (a) {1, 2, 3, ...} (b) {..., −1, 0, 1, 2, ...}
(c) Some out of {parallelogram, trapezium, kite, rhombus, rectangle, square, arrowhead...}
(d) {$x \to x$, $x \to k-x$, $x \to k/x$, ...} (You may have put specific values for k, and you may have remembered some of the more complicated ones such as
$$x \to 1 - \frac{1}{1-x}!)$$

3 See Figure A. $A \cap B = \{1, 3\}$, $A \cup C = \{1, 2, 3, 4, 8\}$

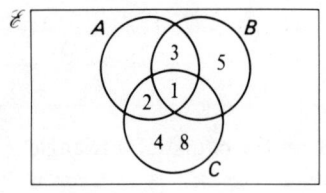 or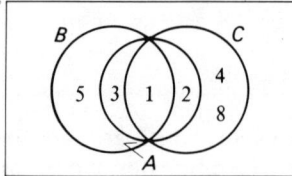

Figure A

4 (a) $\begin{bmatrix}1 & -2\\-3 & 5\end{bmatrix}$ (b) is the same as (a)

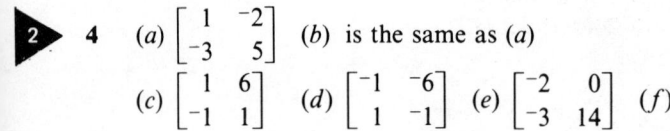

5 (a) $f: x \to x/4$, $g: x \to x+3$, $fg: x \to (x+3)/4$, $gf: x \to x/4+3$
   (b) $f(7) = 1\frac{3}{4}$, $g(7) = 10$, $fg(7) = 2\frac{1}{2}$, $gf(7) = 4\frac{3}{4}$, $f^{-1}(7) = 28$, $g^{-1}(7) = 4$

5.1 Elements, operations and relations

1 Statement (b) is nonsense.
2 Statement (d) is incomplete.
3 Matrices are the elements of matrix algebra.

Exercise A

1 Fractions (rational numbers), real numbers, even and odd numbers, positive integers, etc.
2 In matrix algebra, the elements are matrices, the basic operations are +, −, ×, and the relations are = and ≠.
3 In transformation algebra, the elements are transformations, for example, rotation, reflection, glide reflection, translation, enlargement, shearing, stretching, etc.
4 In number algebra, the operations are +, −, ×, ÷, 'find the highest common factor', 'find the lowest common multiple', etc. There are also unary operations 'square', 'find the square root', 'find the reciprocal', etc. See the next subsection.
5 In set algebra, two operations are ∩ and ∪, and some relations are =, ⊂, and ⊃.
6 (a) See Figure B. (b) Figure 1(a) 'is less than', Figure 1(b) 'is a factor of'

'is greater than'

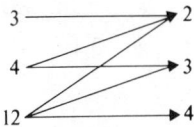

Figure B

7 (a) < or ≠ (b) < or ≠ (c) = (d) ⊂
  (e) = (f) = (g) ≠ (h) ⊂

Operations

1 Other unary operations are 'square', 'cube', 'take the integral part of' ($|3\frac{1}{4}| = 3$), 'find the sin/cos/tan of'; in set algebra, 'find the complement of'; and in matrix and transformation algebra, 'find the inverse of'.
2 (a) +, − (b) +, −, × (c) 'followed by'
  (d) 'followed by' (e) ∩, ∪

Exercise B

1 (a) + (b) 'to the power of' (∗ where $a * b = a^b$)
  (c) ∩ (d) ∪ (e) − (f) − (g) + (h) ÷
2 (a) 3 (b) 8 (c) $9\frac{1}{2}$ (d) 1 (e) 4 (f) 0
  (g) In general, $a * b \neq b * a$.

3 (a) 2 (b) 4 (c) 0 (d) 0 (e) 4 # 2 = 32 (f) 2 # 2 = 8
(g) 3 (h) ⁻9 (i) 3 # 2 = 18 (j) ⁻1 # 18 = 18
(k) It is sometimes true that $a \# b = b \# a$ (as in parts (c) and (d)), but not always (see parts (a) and (b)).
(l) It is sometimes true that $(a \# b) \# c = a \# (b \# c)$ (as in parts (i) and (j)), but not always (see parts (e) and (f)).

4 (a) $fg: x \to 2(x+1)$, $gf: x \to 2x+1$
(b) The operation is 'followed by'.
(c) The elements of this algebra are functions.

5.2 Commutativity, associativity and closure

Commutativity and rearrangement

1 (a) $\begin{bmatrix} 19 & 22 \\ 43 & 50 \end{bmatrix}$ and $\begin{bmatrix} 23 & 34 \\ 31 & 46 \end{bmatrix}$ (b) Both answers are $\begin{bmatrix} 6 & 8 \\ 10 & 12 \end{bmatrix}$.

2 (a) $4+3 = 3+4$ (b) $4-3 \neq 3-4$ (c) $2^3 \neq 3^2$
(d) $5 \times 6 = 6 \times 5$ (e) $5 \div 6 \neq 6 \div 5$ (f) $A \cap B = B \cap A$ (g) $A \cup B = B \cup A$
(h) $[x \to 3x+2$ followed by $x \to 2x] \neq [x \to 2x$ followed by $x \to 3x+2]$

Exercise C

1 Operations (a), (e) and (f) are commutative.
2 (a) $8-3$ is the same as $⁻3+8$, but is not equal to $3-8$.
(b) $15-23$ equals $⁻23+15$, but not $23-15$.
Subtraction is not commutative ($8-3 \neq 3-8$), but addition is. So if we consider $8-3$ as $8+(⁻3)$, this latter form can be rearranged to give $(⁻3)+8$, or $⁻3+8$, which therefore is equal to $8-3$.

Associativity

1 (a) Both equal 15. (b) Both equal 24.
(c) $36 \div (6 \div 3) = 36 \div 2 = 18$, whereas $(36 \div 6) \div 3 = 6 \div 3 = 2$
(d) $(3^4)^2 = 3^4 \times 3^4 = 3^8$, whereas $3^{(4^2)} = 3^{16}$
(e) Both are equal to $\begin{bmatrix} 24 & 28 \\ 87 & 104 \end{bmatrix}$.

2 See Figure C.

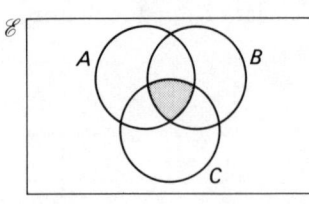
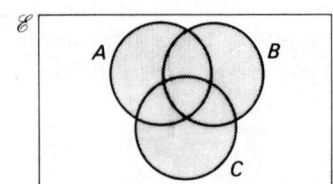

(a) $(A \cap B) \cap C = A \cap (B \cap C)$ (b) $(A \cup B) \cup C = A \cup (B \cup C)$

Figure C

3 (a) $36 \div 4 \div 3 = 9 \div 3 = 3$ (b) $45 - 17 + 6 = 28 + 6 = 34$

Closure

1   Both of these sets are closed.
    In (a), $\dfrac{a}{b} \div \dfrac{c}{d} = \dfrac{a}{b} \times \dfrac{d}{c} = \dfrac{ad}{bc}$, which is still a fraction.
    (As the set contains only *positive* integers, none of a, b, c or d is 0.)
    In (b), if n and m are positive integers, then nm is still a positive integer.

Exercise D

1   (a) $5 * 3 = 11$ and $1 * 8 = 17$
       $(p*q)*r = (p+2q)*r = (p+2q)+2r = p+2q+2r$ and
       $p*(q*r) = p*(q+2r) = p+2(q+2r) = p+2q+4r$
    (b) This operation is not commutative. In general $a+2b \neq b+2a$.
       The work above shows that it is not associative.
    (c) The set is closed under this operation. In fact, the set of real numbers is closed under most operations (one exception is 'find the square root', for $\sqrt{-1}$ is not a real number).

2   (a) $\begin{bmatrix} \tfrac{1}{2} \\ 3 \end{bmatrix}$ (b) $\begin{bmatrix} 2\tfrac{1}{2} \\ 3 \end{bmatrix}$ (c) $\begin{bmatrix} 4 \\ 3\tfrac{1}{2} \end{bmatrix}$

    (d) $(\mathbf{p}*\mathbf{q})*\mathbf{r} = \begin{bmatrix} \tfrac{1}{2} \\ 3 \end{bmatrix} * \begin{bmatrix} 2 \\ 3 \end{bmatrix} = \begin{bmatrix} 1\tfrac{1}{2} \\ 4\tfrac{1}{2} \end{bmatrix}$ (e) $\mathbf{p}*(\mathbf{q}*\mathbf{r}) = \begin{bmatrix} -1 \\ 2 \end{bmatrix} * \begin{bmatrix} 4 \\ 3\tfrac{1}{2} \end{bmatrix} = \begin{bmatrix} 1 \\ 3\tfrac{3}{4} \end{bmatrix}$

    This operation is not commutative, and not associative. The set of 2×1 vectors is closed under this operation, as the result is still a 2×1 vector.

5.3 Identity and inverse elements

The identity element

1   (a) $A \cup \emptyset = \emptyset \cup A = A$ (b) $\emptyset \cup B = B \cup \emptyset = B$
    (c) $\mathscr{E} \cap A = A \cap \mathscr{E} = A$ (d) $B \cap \mathscr{E} = \mathscr{E} \cap B = B$

2   (a) Both equal $\begin{bmatrix} 3 & 2 \\ 1 & 1 \end{bmatrix}$.   (b) Both equal $\begin{bmatrix} 0 & 3 \\ 3 & 0 \end{bmatrix}$.

    (c) Both equal $\begin{bmatrix} 1 & 2 & 3 \\ 4 & 5 & 6 \end{bmatrix}$.   (d) Both equal $\begin{bmatrix} -2 \\ 4 \\ 16 \end{bmatrix}$.

3   The identity for real numbers under $\times$ is 1.
4   $x - 0 = x$ but $0 - x \neq x$. There is no true identity for numbers under subtraction.
5   (a) 1 (b) 1 (c) 1 (d) 1 (e) 6 (f) 1 (g) 48
    There is no identity for this operation.

Inverse elements

1   All four products give the identity matrix $\begin{bmatrix} 1 & 0 \\ 0 & 1 \end{bmatrix}$.

2   (a) $f^{-1}: x \to x/3$, $g^{-1}: x \to x+10$ (b) $f^{-1}f: x \to x$ (c) $ff^{-1}: x \to x$
3   (a) The identity is 1.
    (b) The inverse of 7 is $\tfrac{1}{7}$.
    (c) The inverse of $\tfrac{1}{2}$ is 2.
    (d) The number 0 has no finite inverse.

Exercise E

1 (a)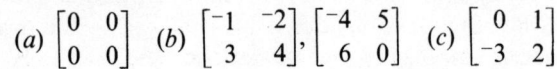

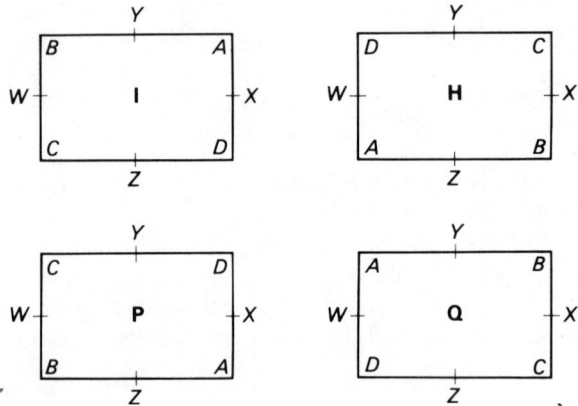

Figure D

2 (a) See Figure D.
  (b) The identity element is **I**.

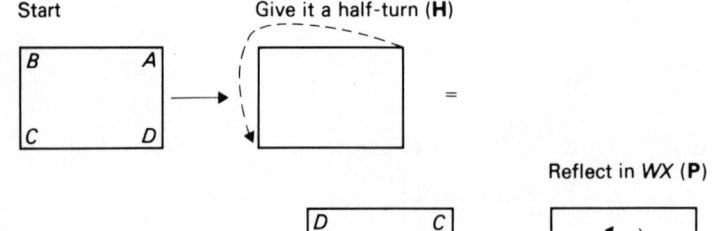

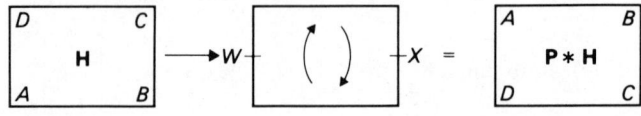

Figure E

(c) **P∗H** means first **H**, then **P**. Figure E shows the effect of this transformation on the rectangle.
    The final position is that given by **Q**, so **P∗H = Q**.
    Similarly **H∗P = Q**, **H∗Q = P**, **Q∗H = P** and **P∗P = I**.

(d) The inverse of **H** is **H**, and the inverse of **P** is **P**. (So they are both self-inverse.)

(e)

*	I	H	P	Q
I	I	H	P	Q
H	H	I	Q	P
P	P	Q	I	H
Q	Q	P	H	I

The only combinations not obtained above are **P∗Q = Q∗P = H**, and **Q∗Q = I**.

(f) As the table is symmetrical about the leading diagonal, the operation is commutative. (It is also associative, as most 'followed by' operations are. Most operations are associative when their combination table is a latin square (every row and every column contains each element of the set once and once only).

3 (a)

'followed by'	$x \to \tfrac{1}{2}x$	$x \to x$	$x \to 2x$	$x \to 2/x$
$x \to \tfrac{1}{2}x$	$x \to \tfrac{1}{4}x$	$x \to \tfrac{1}{2}x$	$x \to x$	$x \to 1/x$
$x \to x$	$x \to \tfrac{1}{2}x$	$x \to x$	$x \to 2x$	$x \to 2/x$
$x \to 2x$	$x \to x$	$x \to 2x$	$x \to 4x$	$x \to 4/x$
$x \to 2/x$	$x \to 4/x$	$x \to 2/x$	$x \to 1/x$	$x \to x$

(b) $x \to x$ is the identity element. (Note that, in the table, the row for the identity element is the same as the row at the top of the table, and the column for the identity element is the same as the column at the left-hand side.)
(c) The inverse of $x \to 2x$ is $x \to \tfrac{1}{2}x$. $x \to 2/x$ is self-inverse.
(d) No ($x \to 4x$, $x \to \tfrac{1}{4}x$ and $x \to 4/x$ are not elements of the original set.)
(e) No (The last row is not symmetrical with the last column.)
(f) Yes (See the note at the end of the section on 'Associativity'.)

4 (a)

$+_4$	0	1	2	3
0	0	1	2	3
1	1	2	3	0
2	2	3	0	1
3	3	0	1	2

(b) 0
(c) 2
(d) 1
(e) Yes
(f) Yes
(g) Yes

(It is lengthy to justify associativity, but the note at the end of the section on 'Associativity' still applies.)

5 (a)

$\times_4$	0	1	2	3
0	0	0	0	0
1	0	1	2	3
2	0	2	0	2
3	0	3	2	1

(b) 1
(c) 2 has no inverse
(d) 3
(e) Yes
(f) Yes
(g) Yes

5.4 The distributive law, and further developments

The distributive law

1 (a) $3 \times 26 = 78$ (b) $24 + 54 = 78$
   (c) $3 + 144 = 147$ (d) $11 \times 21 = 231$
2 (a) and (b) are the same, and would remain so with a different set of numbers.

95

23 3 See Figure F.
    4 Figure F(b) and (d) show that the operation ∩ is distributive over the operation ∪.

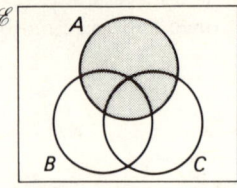
(a) A is shaded

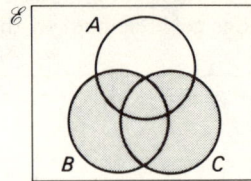
B ∪ C is shaded

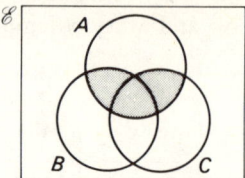
(b) A ∩ (B ∪ C) is shaded

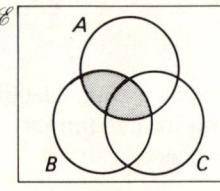
(c) A ∩ B is shaded

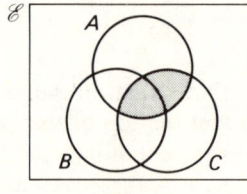
A ∩ C is shaded

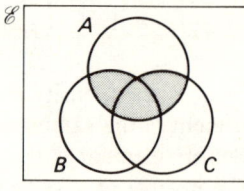
(d) (A ∩ B) ∪ (A ∩ C) is shaded

Figure F

The use of the implication sign

24 1 ⇒ is a relation.
    2 (a) Yes. If $x = 3$, then $x^2 = 9$.
       (b) Since $(^-3)^2 = 9$ as well as $3^2 = 9$, if $x^2 = 9$ then x could be $^+3$ or $^-3$. A correct statement would be $[x^2 = 9] \Leftrightarrow [x = {}^+3 \text{ or } x = {}^-3]$.

Exercise F

25 1 (a) $5 \times 10 + 5 \times 11 = 50 + 55$ (b) $4a + 4b$ (c) $5x + 4x$
       (d) $5x + x^2$ (e) $5x + 5y$ (f) $2 \times 10 + 2 \times 4b = 20 + 8b$
       (g) $4x - x^2$ (h) $8b^2 + b$
    2 (a) $(A \cup B) \cap (A \cup C)$ (b) $(A \cap B) \cup (A \cap C)$
       (c) $(A \cap B) \cup C = C \cup (A \cap B) = (A \cup C) \cap (B \cup C)$
       (d) $(A \cup B) \cap C = C \cap (A \cup B) = (A \cap C) \cup (B \cap C)$
       The operations are commutative, hence parts (c) and (d) can be rearranged as above.
    3 (a) $3(a+b)$ (b) $a(5+6)$ (c) $3(a+2b)$ (d) $x(1+a)$
       (e) $4(2+b)$ (f) $a(b+c)$ (g) $x(9-x)$ (h) $2x(2-x)$
    4 (a) ⇐ (b) ⇔ (c) ⇒ (d) ⇐ (e) ⇒
       A fuller relation for (d) is $[(x+4)(x-3) = 0] \Leftrightarrow [x = 3 \text{ or } x = {}^-4]$.

Post-test

26 1 Elements: 3, x, 1, 7
       Operations: × (implied), +
       Relations: =, ⇒, >
       Punctuation: [, (,),]
    2 The following are possible examples.
       (a) $10 - 3 \neq 3 - 10$ (b) $(12-5) - 2 \neq 12 - (5-2)$ (c) $4 - 7 = {}^-3 \notin I$

3 (a)

A

$\times_{12}$	1	2
1	1	2
2	2	4

B

$\times_{12}$	4	8
4	4	8
8	8	4

C

$\times_{12}$	2	4	8
2	4	8	4
4	8	4	8
8	4	8	4

D

$\times_{12}$	1	5	7	11
1	1	5	7	11
5	5	1	11	7
7	7	11	1	5
11	11	7	5	1

(b) Sets B, C and D are closed under $\times_{12}$.
(c) The identity for A is 1, that for B is 4, C has none, and D has identity 1.
(d) Set A: 1 is self-inverse. 2 has no inverse.
   Set B: 4, 8 are self-inverse.
   Set C: 2, 4, 8 have no inverses.
   Set D: 1, 5, 7, 11 are self-inverse.
(e) Set D under $\times_{12}$ is a group. It is closed, has an identity, and every element has an inverse.

4 (a) $\sqrt{9} = 3$, $\sqrt{16} = 4$, $\sqrt{(9+16)} = 5$, $\sqrt{(9 \times 16)} = 12$
   (b) $\sqrt{(9+16)} \neq \sqrt{9} + \sqrt{16}$, so $\sqrt{}$ is not distributive over addition.
   (c) $\sqrt{(9 \times 16)} = \sqrt{9} \times \sqrt{16}$, which suggests that $\sqrt{}$ could be distributive over multiplication.

Published by the Press Syndicate of the University of Cambridge
The Pitt Building, Trumpington Street, Cambridge CB2 1RP
32 East 57th Street, New York, NY 10022, USA
296 Beaconsfield Parade, Middle Park, Melbourne 3206, Australia

© Cambridge University Press 1981

First published 1981

Printed in Great Britain at the
University Press, Cambridge

British Library cataloguing in publication data
School Mathematics Project
Individualised mathematics.
Algebra 1: Language and structure
1. Mathematics – 1961–
I. Title   II. National Extension College
510   QA39.2   80–49964
ISBN 0 521 23368 2